To a very special family and
my wish for your soul to prosper!

Archie Morran
Proverbs 3:5-6

Soul Survival

Dr. Archie Norman

AuthorHouse™
1663 Liberty Drive
Bloomington, IN 47403
www.authorhouse.com
Phone: 1-800-839-8640

First published by AuthorHouse 7/27/2011

ISBN: 978-1-4567-6341-1 (e)
ISBN: 978-1-4567-6342-8 (hc)
ISBN: 978-1-4567-6340-4 (sc)

Library of Congress Control Number: 2011907978

Printed in the United States of America

This book is printed on acid-free paper.

I am happy to recommend the book, *Soul Survival*, by my good friend Pastor Archie Norman. His fresh insight as a skilled teacher and experienced pastor makes this a great read for anyone interested in a healthy spiritual life.

Tom Messer
Trinity Baptist Church
Jacksonville, Florida

Pastor Norman has gone to great lengths in sharing with us a book that will be a great help to laymen and pastors alike in years to come. The illustrations in this book are so heart written and revealing, and the scriptural approach of healing and regaining spiritual stability is so clear. I endorse this book and commend Pastor Norman for his study, prayer and burden to help God's people. May God add His blessings and grace upon this book in the days ahead.

Don Richards
Pastor – Corinth Baptist Church
President – Baptist Institute of America & Seminary
Loganville, Georgia

Finally, a book that contains some much needed counsel and wisdom and it comes from the heart of a great pastor. His education and experience are noted on every page and his shepherd's heart is quite obvious. The real life experiences that he describes are carefully explained and the biblical explanations that are provided are right on target. The book is filled with expository teaching on the "intricate make-up" of man. Body, soul and spirit are often misunderstood in today's world of counseling. The individuals described herein are but a sampling of what a pastor faces on a daily and weekly basis. Soul talk is necessary, and the author had done a phenomenal job drawing spiritual truth and solid foundational biblical principles into the struggles that everyone faces in life. The book, in my opinion, is a must read for this in ministry. Read it and be blessed.

Dr. Ed Sears
Grace Baptist Temple
Winston-Salem, North Carolina

Archie Norman's writing of *Soul Survival* has revealed some of the depth of his thinking as well as the scope of his knowledge of the Word of God. As an itinerant evangelist/missionary I seldom get to sit in a service and hear sermons. Some pastors send me copies of their church services and I hear them while traveling. Archie Norman's preaching has always ministered to me. This book, like his preaching, is both probing and practical. He has the ability to clarify and to apply theological truth to life situations. I heartily recommend this book. In fact, I could wish that I had written it! May the Lord give it wide distribution.

Dr. Glenn Mathews
Revival Crusade Ministries
Charleston, West Virginia

Soul Survival is an insightful look into the windows of the soul. Many believers today struggle with the issues of life because of a lack of understanding regarding the soul and their "True" Identity in Christ. The book you have in your hand has the potential to lead you to true freedom in Christ.

Phil Mason
Safe Place Ministries
Blairsville, Georgia

I have read the book, *Soul Survival*, by my dear pastor friend and Board member, Dr. Archie Norman. Dr. Norman has obviously spent many hours of research along with his personal experiences of a local church pastor. It has encouraged me greatly that someone has taken the time to answer many difficult questions involved in the ministry. We often dodge these issues with our pet clichés. However, this book draws us to the very core of Christianity and salvation. I am endorsing this book for two reasons. First, I strongly believe in Dr. Norman's commitment to our Lord Jesus Christ, and second, his heartfelt desire for reality in the lives of God's people.

Dr. Jack Reiss
Baptist World Missionary Outreach Ministries, Inc.

I believe this book will be a great help to people in understanding their identity in Christ, and the path to greater and greater godliness. It will also cause many to realize that the answer to their struggles is in Christ and His Word and not their therapist and his counseling sessions. Dr. Norman has carefully guided people back to the sufficiency of Christ and

His truth to provide for all things that pertain to life and godliness. What IS crucial, and what Dr. Norman has so wonderfully conveyed in this book is that God, through Christ, His Spirit and His Word has given us all the resources we need for healing, deliverance and victory.

Dr. Sam Polson
West Park Baptist Church
Knoxville, Tennessee

DEDICATION

To my loving wife Kim, who has been my mainstay through the ups and downs of ministry.

CONTENTS

ACKNOWLEDGMENTS

Some men who are multi-gifted are excellent preachers, talented musicians, and prolific writers. I am not of that number, so I am thankful to those who were willing to assist to make this book possible. Amy Pace is a loyal friend and talented lady who helped by poring over my writing for hours on end in the editing process. No matter how many revisions, she constantly encouraged me that the things in this book would be helpful to others. In addition my assistant, Rebecca Watkins, dedicated so much time in formatting and performing corrections for which I am grateful.

Of course, I must mention all the folks who trusted me enough through the years to open up and share their struggles. It is never easy for those who are in crisis and facing the consequences of poor choices to really come and lay that baggage out for someone else. Often their stories opened up new insights to the Scriptures that helped me in discovering how to experience soul prosperity and joy. It is my prayer that many others will find peace in their souls through these truths.

IS THE SOUL BROKEN?

I can barely function on a day-to-day basis without tears and overwhelming depression. Often I lie in the bed or on the couch while my two small children play and fend for themselves. At times I wonder if life is really worth living.

Sharon

My teen has run away, is strung out on drugs, and is living under a bridge. I remember when he prayed as a little fellow to receive Christ in the back seat of our car with tears running down his little cheeks. I never dreamed it would turn out like this.

Roy

When I was 10 my neighbor began sexually molesting me and yet I made no effort to stop him. Now as an adult he still comes around wanting to continue the relationship. I cannot even confront what he did to me and how it has destroyed my life. Why am I so messed up?

Sandra

Cocaine is about to cost me my wife and little girl. I must stop. Lord, please forgive me for allowing this sin to dominate my life and please set me free in Jesus name.

Bill

Bill left the office with the intent of going home to beg his wife's forgiveness, but stopped at a crack house and spent a week staying high.

I have a problem. I sleep with different men: coworkers, business associates, even strangers. It makes no sense to risk my marriage and endanger my health, but I cannot stop. What am I going to do because I cannot continue to play the hypocrite?

Phyllis

I am not sure if I even have a relationship with the Lord. I have been struggling with feelings of homosexuality for years and I finally caved to the desire. The person I hooked up with is also a member of my church.

Bill

All of these are true encounters I have had in the ministry of counseling at the local church level. Each one had the common experience of claiming that there was a point in time when he/she had received Jesus Christ as Savior and most had been very active in the church. Reading their confessions on the pages of a book cannot accurately portray the anguish of soul as they tearfully tried to come to their pastor for help.

Perhaps I know your thoughts. Come on, these testimonies could not possibly be Christians. They must be mere pretenders who soothe their lost souls with a touch of religion, not sincere followers of the Jesus Christ of the Bible. You make a valid point and probably have a few dozen verses to back up your theory. Yet, could you be wrong?

One thing they all had in common was misery. They were not in my office to gloat about sin, and it was not exactly easy to uncover the darker side of their lives that they were trying so hard to conceal from the rest of the world. Most of them had made personal effort to change their behavior and even sought relief from other resources only to end up in failure. I have to leave my personal conclusions out and commit them to the One who really knows their eternal destiny.

I am more interested in the big question, "Is there a path to a healthy inner person?" Do I have something to offer them that can solve their problem, or am I faced with a dilemma that is over my head and I need to refer them to the "professionals"? Am I stuck with clichés like, "Just trust the Lord," or "We just really need to pray that the Lord will deliver you."

It reminds me of a good friend of mine who was manic depressive and had been under a psychiatrist care for five years. Twice a month she shelled out

$125 to talk about her problem and get another prescription. She was not yet cured when she announced to me that she had to find another doctor because her therapist was temporarily leaving his practice to undergo therapy. It brought new meaning to "physician, heal thyself".

Forgive the slam. This book is not written with the motive of attacking professional counselors or to malign the need for medications. It is a search to find God's answers for the problems of life, both large and small. It is based on the assumption that complex problems have simpler cures when God intervenes. The following certainties apply:

- *Only God can fix a person.*
    - A mechanic may be able to diagnose a car problem and make the necessary repairs, but when it comes to people, the problem is always God-sized and demands Divine intervention.
- *What God does is always against human reasoning.*
    - There is always the "wow" factor. If you can find your own solution, there is no need for God. In fact, the problem is there so you will need Him.
- *God does not need or want our help.*
    - This truth is so difficult for human nature to accept because it attacks pride. God demands faith that looks to Him for answers and relies on Him to work on our behalf.
- *God is an Internist.*
    - Internists are specially trained to solve puzzling diagnostic problems and can handle severe chronic illnesses and situations where several different illnesses may strike at the same time. They also bring to patients an understanding of wellness (disease prevention and the promotion of health)... *Wikipedia*

Every problem is a complicated mixture of spiritual, mental, and physical symptoms which cannot always be discerned by mortals. Throwing a pill at the problem or placing a bandage on the wound may mask the symptoms for a while, but they only serve to prolong the inevitable. Nor do age-old platitudes such as "just get in the Word more," or "well just trust in the

Lord," bring the answer for these struggling individuals. When God takes over and begins to do soul work, He attacks the root cause rather than providing a Band Aid for temporary relief.

The missing piece of the puzzle in examining people's struggles is often the unique dynamic of the human soul. When God formed Adam, He breathed into him the breath of life and man became a *living soul.* The soul is the inner man that gives us our individuality and is the seat of our thoughts, affections, and choices. The unique blend of will, mind, and emotions is at work in creating our problems and is key to overcoming our problems. The Scriptures give insight to the serious nature of this struggle by describing it as warfare and warns of the high cost if we lose the battle of the soul.

> *Beloved, I beg you as sojourners and pilgrims, abstain from fleshly lusts which war against the soul. (I Peter 2:11)*

Reminding the readers that they are just passing through this world to their true home, Peter warns about the conflict they will face. The desires of the flesh will damage the soul. Remember that the flesh wants to provide for, promote, and protect itself rather than die and trust God for its needs. The flesh wants to be the dominant control of the soul which will hinder the mind from being renewed and will cause the heart to love other things in place of God.

Notice that this battle is specifically against the soul, not the spirit or body, and is ongoing throughout the Christian life. When we read the words "fleshly lusts" in the English language, it is impossible not to think of something that is either immoral or extremely evil. The fact is fleshly lusts are any thought or action contrary to the Truth that attempts to satisfy its own needs which then interferes with the soul's purpose of knowing and loving God.

My neighbor, Larry, is a great guy but he has one annoying hobby. If he is home, he is going to be working in his yard and the result is something straight from the pages of Better Homes and Gardens. Once I got a pair of binoculars to see if I could spot a weed coming up through Larry's carpet of Bermuda sod. Not a chance because eagle eye Larry gets it first.

Now this is a real problem for me because, at last count, I have three different kinds of grasses in my yard and that does not include moss, clover, and ordinary weeds! Not to make excuses, but I am a busy Pastor and yard work is not high on my priority list. Fortunately, Larry keeps a well-manicured wooded area between our houses, but you still notice the distinct difference.

My friend has taught me a valuable lesson about weeds. You have to get them up by the roots and replace them with what you want to grow. Such is the problem of fleshly lusts. Left to themselves they choke out our love for Christ and bring destruction to the soul. The Apostle James then lets us see the consequences to the soul if these sinful desires grow unchecked.

> *Brethren, if anyone among you wanders from the truth, and someone turns him back, let him know that he who turns a sinner from the error of his way will save a soul from death and cover a multitude of sins. (James 5:19-20)*

There are some things which deserve clarification. James is speaking directly to Christians about one of their own living in sin. The urgent need is for someone to get that person turned around for the sake of the person's *soul,* his inner well-being. The question is, "What does the word 'death' mean"?

Some would suggest that it is referring to physical death but that would imply that a born-again person could risk losing his soul and face judgment. This is so contrary to what we know about the sufficiency of the work of Christ in salvation which guarantees eternal life. In addition, physical death does not make sense in this context. Would it not seem logical if he was speaking of physical death that James would use the word body or person in place of soul?

Remember the definition of soul from the Bible. The soul consists of the mind where we think and reason, the heart which is the seat of the emotions, and the flesh (will) where the choices of life are made. Through this definition, the Scripture would indicate that a person's soul is dying when the person is unable to think, feel, or choose as God intended. For instance, when a person declares, "I feel like I am *dying inside,*" he is actually telling the truth. Anxiety, depression, anger, bitterness, and lust are just a few of the examples of a soul headed towards death in this life. Many would declare that it is mental illness when the truth is people are suffering in the soul.

These problems cause a loss of passion for God and leave the inner person empty and forlorn. He may attempt to mask the symptoms with alcohol and drugs, pleasure and material wealth, or even recognition through intense Christian service. Every mental or emotional problem the believer faces is the result of an unhealthy soul. When we witness this meltdown in the life of a Christian, we are puzzled by the great contradiction between what the person believes and espouses to others versus the behavior which is so anti-Christian. What is often overlooked is that this person, whose spirit is saved, is losing in the spiritual warfare for his soul.

H.G. Spafford was a lawyer who worked alongside D.L. Moody to help the homeless and suffering in Chicago after the great fire of 1871. Two years later his family decided to take a vacation in Europe where Moody was holding a crusade. Mr. Spafford was delayed by business so his wife and four daughters left on the ship, *Ville de Havre*, with the intent that they would unite later on the other side of the Atlantic.

Off the coast of Newfoundland, the ship collided with an English sailing vessel and sank within 20 minutes. Miraculously, Mrs. Spafford was one of only 47 survivors, but their four daughters, Maggie, Tanetta, Annie, and Bessie perished. Anna Spafford sent her husband a two-word telegram, "Saved alone." Soon the Spaffords had a personal meeting with D.L. Moody where H.G. quietly whispered, "It is well, the will of God be done."

It is impossible to comprehend how a loving father in such deep grief could pen the famous words of this beloved hymn:

When peace like a river attendeth my way;
When sorrows like sea billows roll;
Whatever my lot, thou hast taught me to say,
It is well; it is well with my soul.

Now begins the search to find healing for the soul. You may not have reached the level of defeat as described in the illustrations earlier in the chapter, but there is a present battle for your soul. Only God can accomplish this healing, and He has provided some markers along the way before arriving at the destination. Warning: This is a painful journey and Satan is a real person who will do all he can to convince you it is not worth the effort, or that soul health is impossible for you. Pray that the Lord will give you grace to ignore the assault and find His true plan for you to experience soul prosperity.

LOOKING INTO THE SOUL

The very title of the book causes it to seem insignificant – III John. From the man who gave the world keen insight into the life of Christ through his portrayal in the Gospel, and his vivid description of the end of all human history in the Revelation, John's small letter to Gaius would seem easy to ignore. But, our curiosity is piqued by John's simple introduction in which he challenges our thinking with a simple wish for his friend to have good physical health even as *his soul is prospering.*

> *Beloved, I pray that you may prosper in all things and be in health, just as your soul prospers. (III John 1:2)*

Would you not like to interview Gaius and question him about the prosperous soul? How did he become successful at achieving a healthy soul? Could he give us special insights to lead us down the path to mental and emotional health? My mind whirls at the thought of an interview between Gaius and Larry King where they search deeply for the criteria necessary for a prosperous soul.

Let us face reality. In this world we have many who are followers of Christ and they outwardly testify of the difference Christ has made in their lives. When you scratch beneath the exterior surface though, you often find a life influenced by various lusts, damaging emotions, and strong doubts. It seems Christianity offers a lifestyle that eludes the grasp of many of its followers. These troubled souls would love to find someone who could lead them to experience the victory that they read about and hear others confess they have achieved.

To fully understand our challenge, it is important to look at what constitutes the whole person. Philosophers and teachers through the ages have attempted to explain the complex nature of an individual. The ancient Greeks believed the soul was responsible for behavior. The verb psycho meant "to blow" so the noun *psyche* came to mean the last blow before death, or the soul (breath) leaving the body.

The Bible adds another dimension to the complex make-up of man. In addition to the body and the soul, a person also is a spirit. I Thessalonians 5:23 gives the clearest description of the entire person when Paul prays for God to sanctify the spirit, soul, and body until the day of Christ. Theologians have debated for centuries whether the soul and spirit can be distinguished, and some believe they are synonymous, but there is no question that both exist.

> *Now may the God of peace Himself sanctify you completely; and may your whole spirit, soul, and body be preserved blameless at the coming of our Lord Jesus Christ. (1 Thessalonians 5:23)*

While spirit, soul, and body all interact, influence each other, and are difficult to dissect because they are so interrelated, it helps us to define them in terms we can understand:

- The *spirit* is the unseen part of an individual that relates to God. The spirit of a person without Christ is dead to God, which renders him incapable of having a relationship with God. The spirit of a person is Godlike and will be unable to be annihilated, which means he will face eternal death if the spirit is not made alive by God.
- The *soul* is the intangible part of a person that gives life and individuality. The Scriptures teach that the soul is guaranteed salvation at the moment of receiving Christ, but it is not yet delivered in this life. James instructs believers to receive the implanted word which is able to save their souls. (James1:21)
- The *body* is the physical component of a person that houses the spirit and soul while on earth. We know our bodies are not delivered at the moment of receiving Christ, but we await the final deliverance in the resurrection when it will be raised incorruptible.

Later, we will examine what the soul experiences when the new birth takes place in the spirit, but we must understand that God's promise of salvation is a package deal which includes spirit, soul, and body. You can view it the following way:

- The spirit is saved
- The soul is being saved
- The body will be saved

The spirit is saved

The spirit of a person is dead to God because of the sin that took place in the Garden of Eden. God warned of this resulting death if man chose to disobey by eating the forbidden fruit.

> *But of the tree of the knowledge of good and evil you shall not eat, for in the day that you eat of it you shall surely die. (Genesis 2:17)*

It is obvious that when Adam sinned, he did not die physically, nor did his soul die. After all, we find Adam and Eve having the ability to reason after the fall, by putting on clothes made from fig leaves, and hiding from God which indicates the soul was very much alive. Yet, at that moment in time, his spirit was dead in its relationship to God, and the sacrifice of an animal was necessary to re-establish a right relationship with God.

This malady passed on to all people; all are now dead in trespasses and sin (Ephesians 2:1), and now the new birth is required to be rightly related to God. (John 3:5) There is a special insight into this truth given in I Corinthians 15:45, "And so it is written, the first Adam was made a living soul: the last Adam (Christ) was made a life-giving spirit." It is through the sacrifice of Christ's life on the cross that a person's spirit can be made alive unto God. Once my spirit is made alive, I am eternally connected to God and can enjoy a relationship with God in this life. The Apostle Paul let us know that the redeemed person is connected to the Lord's eternal Spirit as one and this is only possible through a relationship to Christ. (I Corinthians 6:17)

The soul is being saved

Now we turn to the question, "How do you define the soul of a person?" We know that the soul is the inner person and our individuality through which we reason, feel, and make decisions. There are terms in the Bible that allow us to consider how the soul operates. Not only must we establish what these entities are, we must also understand how they function if we are ever to experience a prosperous soul.

The Scriptures reveal three aspects of the soul as it relates to the inner workings of an individual:

1. The *mind*, where all thoughts, reasoning, and intellect occur. It contains everything that has ever been learned or happened to the person in a lifetime. Some of those things seem long forgotten but they remain and influence in big and small ways what a person believes.

2. The *flesh*, the earthly nature of man that is apart from divine influence and through which a person makes the choices and decisions of life. The flesh governs the will of a person and will continue to govern the Christian after salvation unless he learns to walk in the Spirit. (Galatians 5:16)

3. The *heart*, the source of all emotions, but most predominantly the emotion of love. This is the portion of the soul that affects a person's mind and flesh in every way. What or who a person loves will consume the person's thoughts and affect that person's choices.

Each of these aspects of the soul is crucial to our well-being and helps to explain our behavior. The heart, of course, is identified throughout the Scriptures as the most important aspect of a healthy soul, but that does not negate the tremendous roles of the mind and flesh.

The present inner person is changed as the mind that was alienated from God is now being renewed, the heart that was deceitful and desperately wicked is made new, and the will is brought into conformity to the Lord's will. There are Christians who believe this is an optional part of salvation and that some will never win the battle of the soul but instead will remain carnal Christians. It would seem questionable that God has the power to save a person from eternal death but is limited in his ability to deliver the soul in this life.

> *But we are not of those who draw back to perdition, but of those who believe to the saving of the soul. (Hebrews 10:39)*

The body will be saved

Indeed the body is guaranteed salvation, but that will not take place until the resurrection. Since flesh and blood cannot inherit the kingdom, God must raise the body as a spiritual body. While no one fully understands what a "spiritual" body is, we know it will be one that is not subject to the ills of the present life including lust, sin, sickness, and death.

It is sown a natural body, it is raised a spiritual body. There is a natural body, and there is a spiritual body. (I Corinthians 15:44)

The sting of death is sin, and the strength of sin is the law. (I Corinthians 15:56)

In our society, Christians would never think that a person was not saved based on the individual's physical condition. Can you imagine hearing, "I do not think that guy is saved since his body is supposed to be the temple of God and he is overweight?" Certainly God would rather we take care of our bodies, but He does not judge a person's salvation based on his/her body. In like manner, a person's failure to prosper in his soul during this present life does not necessarily indicate the person will miss heaven because he is not prospering in his soul.

Here is another way to view this great subject in simple terms:

- The **spirit** is saved in this present world from the **penalty** of sin.
- The **soul** is **being saved** in this present world from the **power** of sin.
- The **body will be saved** after this present world from the **presence** of sin.

For the most part, believers can readily understand through the eyes of faith the salvation of the spirit and even accept the salvation of the body without much confusion. But, the salvation of the soul is where we stumble since we cannot comprehend that the Lord desires to save the inner person in this life. Before the soul can be healthy, a person must come into a proper relationship with God through an event that took place almost two thousand years ago.

SOUL WORK AND SPIRIT RESURRECTION

Most religions mention the importance of the soul in some manner, but Christianity is the only faith that teaches the soul cannot be healthy until the spirit of the person is resurrected. God's revelation is that a person is dead in sin (Ephesians 2:1), and unless there is a supernatural event in the life, a relationship with God does not exist. This action, which confuses so many people in the world and is the subject of ridicule, is called the new birth and implies that a spiritual birth must take place in addition to physical life.

Nearly thirty years ago, a little known Democratic governor burst onto the American political scene and became the first President from the Deep South elected since Zachary Taylor in 1848. Taking advantage of the Watergate scandal and people's natural distrust of politicians, Jimmy Carter used his amiable personality and his promise to be as competent and compassionate as the American people to become President. For the first time, faith became a prominent theme as President Carter proudly declared himself to be a born-again Christian.

While many Americans since that time have discussed the subject, there is still great division regarding what the term "born again" means. Most relate the term to accepting Jesus Christ as personal Savior but there seems to be an ignorance concerning Biblical truth and the new birth. No greater evidence reveals this uncertainty more than the fact that 54% of Americans believe that a person can go to heaven if he is generally good or does good things. (www.barna.org/beliefs/salvation)

What did Jesus mean that night as Nicodemus, a respected ruler of the Jews, came to address Him as "Teacher?" His command, "You must be born again," created an avid curiosity in the heart of Nicodemus and brought to him a perplexing confusion concerning this phrase which he tried to understand in physical terms. What we discover in Scripture is that the new birth is a "soul work" that brings life to the spirit of a person who is dead in trespasses and sin.

The must of the new birth

In the real world, we believe there is an exception to every rule. After all, there are always extenuating circumstances and other factors that lead us to believe that rules are made to be broken. With the word "must" Jesus seemed to close all the loop holes and make it an open and shut case that this is the ticket to heaven. No exceptions. Why?

Humans have a problem they are reluctant to face. The problem is that in our natural state we are totally alienated from God. The Bible paints a very bleak picture of the natural man that most people are unwilling to accept. The natural man is a descendent of the first Adam and is the recipient of Adam's corrupt, condemned sinful nature. In Adam, "all died" (I Corinthians 15:22), and the result is that every human is dead to God, a servant to sin, and lives to satisfy the desires of the flesh.

> *And you He made alive, who were dead in trespasses and sins, in which you once walked according to the course of this world, according to the prince of the power of the air, the spirit who now works in the sons of disobedience, among whom also we all once conducted ourselves in the lusts of our flesh, fulfilling the desires of the flesh and of the mind, and were by nature children of wrath, just as the others. (Ephesians 2:1-3)*

He is under the wrath of God and will never satisfy God through religious or moral effort.

> *So then, those who are in the flesh cannot please God. (Romans 8:8)*

These Biblical facts fly in the face of human reasoning and man's opinion of himself. Most people confront these problems with a nonsensical belief that states everyone has a spark of goodness that needs to be kindled. A person is innately good and society's problems, such as lack of education or poverty, cause them to go bad. Solve a person's physical and emotional needs, and the person will be a productive member of society. Like Nicodemus, many think in physical terms instead of the spiritual.

Even the followers of Christ have become weak on this message. While acknowledging that sin is a problem that must be addressed, the facts are often softened. The emphasis of the Christian message has become, "You have done something wrong (sin), but the important thing is to pray and ask Jesus to save you." In this presentation, there is little sense of guilt or condemnation that would lead to a mental assent to the Gospel (Jesus' death, burial, and resurrection). The question is whether such confession is actually the new birth about which Jesus taught.

Unfortunately, in our quest to have people embrace the Gospel we have short-circuited the process. We have seriously ignored Jesus' requirement for repentance in the matter of salvation. In Luke 13:3, Christ clearly states "unless you repent, you will all likewise perish," but we have substituted repentance with a general knowledge about sin, along with a reminder to "tell Him you are sorry." Only when a person sees his true condition from the Biblical perspective as revealed by the Holy Spirit, will he be driven to see the love of the cross and to cry out in faith as he sees the substitution of Christ as his only hope.

The mystery of the new birth

Everyone loves a mystery, especially if the mystery is solved and we understand the outcome in the end. With the new birth, that is not so easy. For a person who has experienced being born again, it is a struggle to express what has taken place in terms that others may understand. The end result is the born-again believer finds great joy in the experience while the unbeliever looks on with skepticism. So, why is being born again such a mystery?

Certainly the word *grace* enters the picture because most people are unprepared when God begins to show them their standing with Him, and allows them to see the true meaning of Calvary. Most Christians give testimony to the sense that God seemed to be reaching out to them through a friend or circumstance that at the moment seemed very unusual. As Saul of Tarsus, they were walking along one day with their own agenda, when Christ in a radical way intervened and brought about drastic transformation. At times the word *grace* seems too simplistic a term to describe God's unusual work.

There is also the factor that the work described in John 3 is *unseen.* Poor Nicodemus sat there going through this vivid picture of a grown man entering back into his mother's womb. How absurd! Jesus is giving him a physical example to demonstrate how an individual enters God's family. The new birth is the mysterious union of the Word of God and the Spirit of God at work in the human heart to produce spiritual life.

The most important truth often overlooked in the study of Nicodemus' encounter with Jesus Christ is that this is a work of the *Spirit* of God in the *spirit* of man. A person's tendency is to relate the new birth to physical or mental terms. Certainly it will affect the mind and body but, first and foremost, it is taking the natural man that is dead to God and making his spirit alive unto God.

The mechanics of the new birth

This may sound like strange terminology when you consider the supernatural aspect of salvation. The new birth is the spirit of man, which is dead to God, being brought to life and then transformed through his soul. The truth of man's condition before God is seen through the prism of his mind, emotions, and will as the Gospel is given to him; as he receives in his soul the good news of Christ's death and resurrection. God miraculously brings life to the spirit in the person.

This is most clearly seen through the first public appeal made after the resurrection of Jesus Christ. A group of people were witnessing on the day of Pentecost and questioning the absurdity of the behavior of the Christians present when Peter stood to preach a sermon. (Acts 2:14-37) God's work in the souls of this multitude of people gives clear insight to the pattern of salvation that would follow throughout the book of Acts.

- The truth explained to the mind - Using Old Testament Scriptures, Peter gave an explanation of this phenomenon and verified that Jesus Christ was the Messiah who suffered death, and then was raised to life. He clearly places the responsibility for Christ's rejection and death at their feet.

"Therefore let all the house of Israel know assuredly that God has made this Jesus, whom you crucified, both Lord and Christ." (Acts 2:36)

This seems to indicate that a mental confrontation with the Gospel must take place in the soul of man before the new birth can ever take place.

So then faith comes by hearing, and hearing by the Word of God. (Romans 10:17)

- The truth felt in the heart -The truth struck home and touched the emotions.

Now when they heard this, they were cut to the heart, and said to Peter and the rest of the apostles, "Men and brethren, what shall we do?" (Acts 2:37)

Their hearts were cut by the awareness of their personal responsibility which led to intense feelings of guilt. Imputed righteousness which God supplies takes place in the heart.

For with the heart one believes unto righteousness, and with the mouth confession is made unto salvation. (Romans 10:10)

- The truth accepted in the flesh -There is a demand for a human response (Acts 2:37). They did not know what to do, but they had a keen awareness that faith would demand action. At this point, no negotiations took place or even careful reflection upon their reaction. The Spirit of God had quickened their spirits and they willingly obeyed the instructions.

Then those who gladly received his word were baptized; and that day about three thousand souls were added to them. (Acts 2:41)

This Biblical pattern of salvation can be seen in other conversions that took place in the book of Acts. The Ethiopian Eunuch was reading the Scripture and as Philip explained the passage, he believed in his heart.

Then Philip opened his mouth, and beginning at this Scripture, preached Jesus to him. (Acts 8:35)

The will was affected when he declared Jesus to be the Son of God and requested baptism.

Then Philip said, "If you believe with all your heart, you may." And he answered and said, "I believe that Jesus Christ is the Son of God." (Acts 8:37)

Even the celebrated conversion of Saul on the road to Damascus contains these truths. Jesus had to reveal to Saul who He was, which then brought about a work in his heart as Saul trembled with emotion and was astonished. Finally the will was affected with a simple question, "What would you have me do?"

And he said, "Who are You, Lord?" Then the Lord said, "I am Jesus, whom you are persecuting. It is hard for you to kick against the goads." (Acts 9:5)

Notice that each part of the soul is affected by this process. The mind understands that my sin caused Christ to die as a substitute in my place, the emotions are touched by this act of undeserving love, and my will chooses to accept this sacrifice of God on my behalf. The Gospel must influence the entire soul of a person to be effective in producing eternal life.

The miracle of the new birth

The miraculous work of the new birth changes everything:

- My relationship with God: I am now accepted by Him and part of His family.

To the praise of the glory of His grace, by which He made us accepted in the Beloved. (Ephesians 1:6)

For you are all sons of God through faith in Christ Jesus. (Galatians 3:26)

- My relationship with Satan: I am no longer in darkness, deceived by him.

He has delivered us from the power of darkness and conveyed us into the kingdom of the Son of His love, (Colossians 1:13)

- My relationship to sin: I am no longer under the authority of sin and my desire towards sin changes.

Certainly not! How shall we who died to sin live any longer in it? (Romans 6:2)

For sin shall not have dominion over you, for you are not under law but under grace. (Romans 6:14)

- My relationship to the world: I am part of Christ's kingdom which is not of this world.

Jesus answered, "My kingdom is not of this world. If My kingdom were of this world, My servants would fight, so that I should not be delivered to the Jews; but now My kingdom is not from here." (John 18:36)

Behold what manner of love the Father has bestowed on us, that we should be called children of God! Therefore the world does not know us, because it did not know Him. (I John 3:1)

- My relationship to judgment: I have escaped the penalty of sin which is separation from God.

"Most assuredly, I say to you, he who hears My word and believes in Him who sent Me has everlasting life, and shall not come into judgment, but has passed from death into life. (John 5:24)

There is therefore now no condemnation to those who are in Christ Jesus, who do not walk according to the flesh, but according to the Spirit. (Romans 8:1)

In order to start on the road to a healthy soul, a person must not only experience the new life created by being born again, but must also be assured in the inner person that this has taken place. There is definite value in receiving eternal life in Christ, but God's goal is for each person to experience abundant life before heaven. Such life is impossible if the person questions his relationship with God.

Jesus warned about many who would one day stand before him in judgment convinced that they were about to enter heaven only to be turned away. (Matthew 7:21-23) What a sad time to figure out that your wrongful determination about the subject of salvation would cause eternal consequences. While many will face this event, you do not have to be one. You can be assured of salvation if you come on God's terms.

There are several forms of assurance that are helpful in reaching the conclusion that you are indeed part of God's family. As these are examined, be careful not to assume you know the answer since both the mind and emotions can be deceived concerning salvation. Often I find people depending on a form of assurance that brings a measure of personal comfort but does not allow them the confidence they need to face the Lord.

Personal assurance based on feelings-II Corinthians 13:5

This assurance results from a person doing a close inspection of the salvation event where he first met Jesus Christ. Usually it is based on a memory of an event that took place in a revival service, a Vacation Bible School, or some other place where he responded to an invitation. For some, this memory is fuzzy because it happened as a child or the details are not easy to remember. At times he may question if the decision was real because of being coerced by a friend or family member, and, in some cases, question if true conviction and repentance took place. In fairness, experiences can be deceptive even though an experience is important to our understanding of being born again.

People assurance based on knowledge-II Timothy 1:5

At times, some testify of Christianity based on the persuasion of others. Certainly others should see something in your life that indicates the new birth has taken place. For some, this can create a false assurance. This may happen as a well-meaning parent continues to relate to his child an incident that took place in the past at home or at church. The parent tries to assure the child that he is saved because of that event. In other cases, it is the individual who pointed the person to Christ that attempts to give him assurance. This has been popularly taught in soul-winning courses in Fundamental and Evangelical circles. Relating facts does not necessarily give a person assurance. Many people testify that they had a false experience or even a false assurance of salvation before truly coming to Christ.

Biblical assurance based on determining a Bible is true-I John 5:13

For those who love the Bible, I almost hear a collective sigh of relief. Yes, this is where real assurance takes place. The Bible said it, I believe it, and that settles it. Could a person give a mental assent to the *facts* of the Gospel? Could a person admit he is a sinner, believe that Jesus died for him, and pray a prayer and not be saved? Before you answer, allow me to give an illustration. As a student in Bible College, I was expected to turn in a weekly report concerning how many people to whom I witnessed and how many conversions took place. It was not unusual, in my zeal, to head down to the street where all the bars were located. I am not proud to say that I "led" many of those drunks to the Lord by getting them to pray the sinner's prayer. Please do not try to convince me the new birth took place because the facts were acknowledged.

In each of these forms of healthy assurance, it can be seen how each targets a particular aspect of the soul.

- It might be a feeling which was produced at the moment of salvation involving the emotions.
- It might be a memory of an event that took place assuring the intellect that a promise had been accepted.
- It might be a determination of the will which decided I did what God said, so now I am saved.

I repeat, while these assurances are healthy, they could be dangerous because the mind, emotions, and will can be deceived. Therefore, God adds a better way.

Spiritual assurance based on the Spirit of God speaking to the spirit of the individual-Romans 8:16

In my experience, this is the most neglected form of assurance. Spiritual assurance is not often taught; it is difficult to define the unseen work of the Spirit in salvation, let alone see it take place in a visible manner after salvation. Yet, it is a very real principle of Scripture even though it is difficult to explain. This assurance comes directly from God. As I read about such assurance in the lives of others, there seems to be a pattern. First, the soul wrestles with personal sinfulness and God's holiness. This often leads to despair because it seems the two could never be reconciled. Finally, the Spirit of God speaks to the heart, sometimes through a Scripture verse, or a song, or even a statement made by another believer. While the source might differ, the truth that brought assurance is always similar: the blood of Jesus Christ is enough, and God is satisfied!

Once a person is saved and receives assurance, two problems must be addressed. First, as discussed earlier, is the understanding that some of the above assurances can be false. A person could give mental assent to the Gospel, or have a tremendous emotional experience at some point in his life without salvation ever taking place. In the same manner, a person could be convinced of a salvation that does not exist even though he knows certain Bible verses. That is why genuine assurance must be the product of God's Spirit convincing your spirit that you know the Lord. A friend of mine is a perfect example of this.

Frank came to me because of a marital problem; his situation required they get help or they were through. Not raised in a Christian home, he had begun to attend church as a teen just to be with his friend. Under the persuasive influence of the Pastor, he had prayed a prayer to receive Christ and even attended a few Bible college classes. Ten years later, he was watching his life unravel and he was not sure why.

As we talked, I kept sensing that the problem was deeper than the fact he had been losing his temper at home and his finances were in shambles. When we discussed salvation, his mental prowess kicked in and he could rattle off all the right answers. When pinned down, there was little evidence of the new birth. So we dealt with the issue of assurance of the Spirit and I sent him home to ask God a question: Am I saved or lost?

He returned three days later for another session. I asked him if God had answered his question, and he replied in the negative. He wanted to start throwing Scripture verses at me but, I simply instructed him to go home and let God reveal to his heart what the answer was. Deep down, I sensed he was not a Christian, but I have been wrong before. I have seen others who sought God for the answer and received full assurance of salvation.

That Sunday night, I noticed Frank slip out while the congregation was singing but paid little attention when he did not return. After the service, he was the first to greet me and asked to speak with me in private. Immediately, he said, "I know the answer. I have been out on the church ball field while you were preaching, and I know I am not a Christian."

In a moment, he was calling out to God in repentance for being a phony and began trusting fully in the work of Christ. I know this may sound crazy, but there was such a drastic difference in him when he stopped praying that he actually looked different. Tears and brokenness were replaced by joy and peace.

Frank has become one of the most changed young men I have ever met. His wife and children were the first to notice, and it was not a moment of temporary insanity. He has become a tremendous witness for Jesus Christ. Several months later, his father-in-law jokingly told me that he could never get Frank to talk about spiritual matters and now he could not get him to shut up!

The second serious problem that often takes place is confusion about how your soul is affected by your new birth into God's family. When a person receives Christ, there is an initial euphoria in every aspect of the soul. The will has surrendered to Christ and there is peace, the mind is convinced that its discovery of the Gospel will never err from truth again, and, of course, the love of Christ which fills the heart is a high that the new Christian is convinced will never pass away. In reality, the battle for the Christian's soul is just beginning.

MAKING DEPOSITS INTO THE SOUL

When my wife and I were newly married I was the Pastor of a very small church, and our funds were very limited. Things were so tight that we shared a vacuum cleaner with the church - I know this sounds pretty much on the verge of poverty. One day I was preparing to head home for lunch, and Kim called to ask if I could bring the vacuum cleaner home for her to use that afternoon. I hung up the phone, headed for the door, and immediately stopped because I knew I was forgetting something…

Twenty-seven years later I still remember the incident, but in that 30 second span I could not recall what my wife had asked me to do (which explains why the mind is a terrible thing to waste). How do you explain recalling something that happened a decade ago, while sometimes you struggle to remember your telephone number?

Remember there was a determination made earlier that the soul can be defined in three categories that make up the inner person:

1. The mind, where all thoughts and reasoning occur, and where information is stored.
2. The flesh, which governs the will and where the decisions and choices of life are made.
3. The heart, which is the source of our emotions, love being the key.

Your mind is a depository

Your mind is a depository that stores *every* piece of information that has entered, and life experience that has ever taken place. Some deposits are repressed, some forgotten, and some cherished. While this information is all stored in the brain, some deposits are easier to recall than others.

Imagine your mind as a vault, and every moment of your life something is being deposited there. Some of the information is so inconsequential we tend to think it entered in one ear and came out the other. There is a sense that it is long forgotten, but it is in the vault whether we want to use it or not. At times the mind seems so full, but another day comes, and magically there is still room for more.

How are these deposits made? First, they come from the experiences of life. You touch a hot stove and a lesson is learned for future encounters. You taste ice cream and the next time you get near the stuff, your mouth begins to salivate. Through experience you learn to walk, ride a bicycle, or drive a car. Everything is stored in your memory and can even become second nature to you. Not all experiences are beneficial and some may actually cause harm. But, they all are stored in the vault.

Also, there are a host of people who influence you and make deposits into the mind. Your mind has been affected by parents, teachers, friends, family and an endless list of lesser known individuals. Some have helped you achieve success and others have plagued you with doubt and fear. People can bring out the best in you or make deposits that cripple you for a lifetime. Some have even placed things in your mind without your permission.

It must not be overlooked that you make more deposits into your mind than all the other facets combined. The input of knowledge through your senses - sight, sound, touch, taste and smell - is all a part of the vault. As you take in the sights and sounds of books, nature, or media, it forever affects your thinking in positive or negative ways.

There is a final, often overlooked way your mind is influenced. The Bible refers to our *imaginations,* which is another way of saying a person's ability to deliberate with himself in his mind. This is when a person takes the information, experience, and influence that he possesses in the mind, and draws conclusions through reasoning. Romans 1:21 declares there was a time in the past where people had a true revelation of God but when "they knew God, they glorified him not as God," which resulted in the people creating a God in their imagination, which led to their hearts being blinded to the True God. Once people fail to accept God's revelation of Himself it leads them to idolatry, the forming of a god in the mind that suits the individual. Paul uses this point to emphasize why every person is guilty before God. (Romans 3:19)

The warning is also issued for the Lord's people to not allow reasoning formed in their own minds to interfere with what they know is true concerning God. Paul warns that believers will be attacked by thoughts that are contrary to the nature of God and they must cast down those arguments that lift themselves up against what God reveals about Himself - "bringing every thought into captivity to the obedience of Christ." (II Corinthians 10:5) The mind is flooded by attacks from the world establishment against truth, as well as conclusions drawn from human experience and questions from what we observe. These false thoughts can attack your faith and create many problems for your soul.

I married into a family that loves the sport of hunting. My father-in-law owned a farm where the family would gather on weekends to hunt. When our children were small, my wife loved for me to sit with her in a blind and wait for a big deer to come by. Needless to say, when my sons were old enough, they both also fell in love with hunting.

I can honestly say I did not enjoy going very much. The first time I shot a deer I was uncertain if I'd actually hit it or not; we never recovered the kill, but we found the carcass decaying a few weeks later. It reminded me of times as a child when my dad would take me squirrel hunting. It seemed I could never see those critters bouncing around in a tree. My dad would get very frustrated at my inability to see the squirrels, and even though he was not critical, it became a very uncomfortable experience for me.

Through these various experiences, I concluded in my mind that I am not a good hunter. This, along with cold frosty mornings in a deer stand or long hours of not seeing a deer pass by, resulted in my increased dislike for hunting. The combination of believing I was not talented at the sport and not deriving pleasure from hunting eventually led me to give up on the idea altogether. On the other hand, if I would have had enjoyable experiences while hunting with my father, it might have completely changed my outlook about hunting.

If you ponder for a while, you will discover that your likes and dislikes are affected by your reasoning from past input. It is all there. Like all of the information on the worldwide web, your mind stores every tidbit of knowledge, every circumstance in your experience, and every way various people have touched your life. These things can help to confirm truth in your mind or they can attack truth in both direct and subtle ways. My brain is on overload just trying to bring this into proper perspective!

Your heart determines the value of the deposit

Once the deposit is made, your heart must determine the value of the information or experience. Even though everyone has a vault of good and bad collections, the heart is the source whereby you decide which to keep. In Luke 6:45, Jesus compares the heart to a place where good and evil treasure is stored. What the heart treasures then leads the person to certain actions. If the deposit results in a good treasure, the result will be good actions while evil treasure will lead to evil behavior. Jesus reaffirms this truth in Matthew 15:19 when He declares, "For out of the heart proceed evil thoughts, murders, adulteries, fornications, thefts, false witness, blasphemies," which cause a person to be defiled.

There are some very important things to remember about this collection of deposits that have been made in the mind throughout a person's lifetime:

- The deposits are good and bad. Some had parents that gave secure discipline and loving instruction while others were verbally or physically abused. Some filled their minds with educational pursuits that led to a good career while others collected smut from magazines and the internet.

- The deposits are true and false. A person may have received positive reinforcements about his abilities and talents while another was told he was only an accident waiting to happen. If someone has been told continually that he is worthless, he will grow up believing it is impossible for God to love him. A lie can become as believable as the truth.

- The deposits are helpful and harmful. "As a man thinks in his heart, so is he" is a profound truth. The deposits made in the mind can produce a President or a serial killer.

The truth of helpful and harmful deposits can be seen in everyone's life to one degree or another. For example my wife teaches second graders and recently she was invited to an event for a former student who was now in the tenth grade. The mother of this young man shared that after all these years my wife was still his favorite teacher. She deposited into this young man a love for learning and belief that he could succeed. Because of my wife's great love for her students and strong discipline in the class room, she has become a favorite of many students.

How often have you seen the exact opposite take place in someone's life? There are children who are constantly beat down by authority figures with verbal assaults or cruel attacks upon their character and abilities. Some enter a shell of incompetence which leads to frustration or failure while others try to break out by all sorts of self-destructive behavior. It is not unusual to see many of these children grow into adulthood on a road to nowhere, prison, or even worse. While each person is responsible for his or her own actions, it does not help to have authorities who cripple by attacking the soul.

Remember that the heart sorts through the collection deposits of the mind according to an emotional response. The "good deposits" result in feelings of joy, security, pleasure, expectation, and other favorable emotions, while the "bad" are burdened by a sense of guilt, anger, fear, depression, etc. These various emotions seek control over the heart in an attempt to find emotional well-being.

Overlooked in this quest for emotional health is the truth that God has established one emotion of the heart to rule over every other mood. God has designed ***love*** to reign supreme in the human heart in three simple ways:

1. Experiencing security in His love by knowing and receiving His love on a constant basis.

   That Christ may dwell in your hearts through faith; that you, being rooted and grounded in love, may be able to comprehend with all the saints what is the width and length

> *and depth and height— to know the love of Christ which passes knowledge; that you may be filled with all the fullness of God. (Ephesians 3:17-19)*
>
> *In this is love, not that we loved God, but that He loved us and sent His Son to be the propitiation for our sins. (I John 4:10)*

2. Demonstrating whole-hearted love for God in my relationship with Him.

> *Hear, O Israel: The LORD our God, the LORD is one! You shall love the LORD your God with all your heart, with all your soul, and with all your strength. (Deuteronomy 6:4-5)*
>
> *Jesus said to him, 'You shall love the LORD your God with all your heart, with all your soul, and with all your mind.'(Matthew 22:37)*

3. Sharing love with everyone in our world.

> *And the second is like it: 'You shall love your neighbor as yourself.' (Matthew 22:39)*
>
> *If you really fulfill the royal law according to the Scripture, "You shall love your neighbor as yourself," you do well; (James 2:8)*

Love becomes the anchor of the soul by which every human motive and action is judged.

> *Though I speak with the tongues of men and of angels, but have not love, I have become sounding brass or a clanging cymbal. And though I have the gift of prophecy, and understand all mysteries and all knowledge, and though I have all faith, so that I could remove mountains, but have not love, I am nothing. And though I bestow all my goods to feed the poor, and though I give my body to be burned, but have not love, it profits me nothing. (I Corinthians 13:1-3)*

God is love; if we are to love properly, it is His love in us that makes that happen. Unfortunately, sin is what deadens our heart to love.

And because lawlessness will abound, the love of many will grow cold. (Matthew 24:12)

Your flesh makes decisions based on what is received from the mind and the heart.

There is an immediate question that results from using the term "flesh" to describe an aspect of the inner person. The word occurs more than 400 times in our English Bible and most often refers to our physical bodies that consist of *flesh and bones.* Even animals are described as having flesh.

On the other hand, the word flesh is used in the New Testament to describe the inward nature of man that seeks its own welfare and benefit apart from God. Romans 8:5 reminds us to know that "those who live according to the flesh set their minds on the things of the flesh, but those who live according to the Spirit, the things of the Spirit." The synonymous term for flesh would be "self," the desire and the right to make my own decisions and control my own life. The flesh is the decision maker of the soul even though it is influenced by the heart and mind. The flesh remains corrupt even after the person receives the Gospel.

You may question why you make many of the choices you make, especially when so many of those decisions lead to your misery. Life unravels when the flesh makes those selections without Divine influence, yet the flesh is convinced of its own wisdom. At the root of the problem is flesh's innate ambition to ensure that physical life arrives at the following goals.

First is the quest for *pleasure* because life is supposed to be enjoyed at any cost. Rich and poor meet together at the stream of happiness. The pursuit of happiness may be sought through material things, relationships, or the dream of various accomplishments. The flesh seeks to make logical choices to allow the individual to arrive at this destiny.

The flesh also is motivated to *protect* itself; it cherishes the physical life.

For no one ever hated his own flesh, but nourishes and cherishes it, just as the Lord does the church. (Ephesians 5:29)

Pain and suffering are unacceptable because they are uncomfortable and harm the flesh. Fleshly choices revolve around making one's self feel better or improving position in life. Those decisions are usually made in spite of the impact on others because "I" am most important.

Finally the goal of *preservation* must be met because when self is in control the present is what matters. The flesh has no comprehension of the eternal. The end of physical life brings an end to the flesh. At the heart of almost every decision is the determination of whether a circumstance or experience will extend life or facilitate an easier time while on earth. At times, these three goals of the flesh conflict with each other and one has to win out.

At first this process of the inner man appears to be simple. By bringing mind, heart, and will into check, one will experience peace. Upon closer examination, however, you find that the process is not simple because everyone is wired differently. Some are governed more by reasoning, some by a strong will, and others by emotional highs and lows. In addition, we enter into our new life in Christ with a lot of baggage from the past. Until the believer is willing to face and deal with those experiences God's way, the prosperity of the soul will be hindered.

THE SOUL'S ATTEMPT TO COPE WITH THE PAST

The term *dysfunctional* has become a very common buzz word in American society. Most people have become aware that things from the past have had a bearing on how we conduct ourselves in the present. For some, past relationships have become an excuse for faulty behavior in the present. Others minimize the idea that the way we were treated in the past has any influence on the present. For Christians this is even more confusing because we are often taught that at the moment of salvation the past mysteriously disappears.

At the time of accepting Christ as Savior, the Christian receives complete forgiveness from God which relieves guilt, but it does not erase all the things that happened in the past and the influence they have on the soul. Without question, the past does affect the present. However, there are varying degrees of reaction to the past according to the individual's temperament and the extent of the problems faced. These negative experiences can be categorized into four major emotions:

- The confusion caused by a dysfunctional life.
- The frustration caused by an insecure life.
- The guilt caused by a sinful life.
- The bitterness caused by an abused life.

For most of us, we are not totally aware of how much the past affects us in the present. It is easier to just suppress those negative experiences and concentrate on the here and now. What about those nagging problems from the past that will not go away? It may be your parents, who seemingly programmed you for failure, with their constant verbal attacks about your looks, abilities, or future chances to make it in life. What about the spouse who led you to believe that you shared the same values and dreams before marriage, but through the years proved to be exactly the opposite person? Even more serious is your memory of the person from the past who robbed you of your innocence and ability to love through sexual abuse.

For some, the past leaves nothing more than perplexing questions that seem to go unanswered. Why is there no justice? Many people are convinced that they did nothing to cause the injustices in their past, and they are left with the sense that life is not fair. They seem to muddle through the present with the idea that the cards are stacked against them and they will never get the break they deserve.

This leads to a much more serious problem in regards to a person's faith. The questions that always seems to surface are: Where was God when I was hurt in the past? Why did He allow certain things to happen when He knew the damage, and was more than able to prevent it from taking place? How can I trust Him in the present when He seemed to be untrustworthy in my past?

Most people reasonably work through these issues and cultivate a faith in the Lord despite the confusing feelings. They fall back on the omniscience and wisdom of God that concludes His thoughts are higher than our human reasoning. It is not that these questions vanish, but the questions are held in check, and they choose not to ponder the depth of their answers.

There is an increasing number of Christians who are not dealing well with a quick-fix answer. With the decline of solid Bible knowledge about God's attributes and little understanding that there is absolute truth, many are drowning in a quagmire of uncertainty. They fail to realize that there are definite consequences for not dealing with their past from a Biblical position.

Before we examine what those consequences are, we need to look at how we attempt to deal with the past in our own ways. In some ways, we have come to believe that our present world has such complex problems, that we conclude the ancient times in which the Bible was written could not possibly assist us in finding solutions. We ignore the Preacher's admonition in Ecclesiastes which reveals that there is "nothing new under the sun."

Our greatest revelation needs to be that human nature never changes. We can learn lessons and gain insights from others in the past who erroneously attempted to solve their problems. Let's examine a few characters in Scripture who tried various methods to conquer their past; we may find that we follow their example.

Esau: I must get over it

From birth, Esau's life was a most unusual one. The first twin out, notwithstanding a brother holding onto his heel, meant he was in line for good things in a covenant household.

- *Physical blessings*

1. Contained a double portion of the family inheritance

    But he shall acknowledge the son of the unloved wife as the firstborn by giving him a double portion of all that he has, for he is the beginning of his strength; the right of the firstborn is his. (Deuteronomy 21:17)

2. Received authority over other members of the family

- *Spiritual blessings*

1. Patriarch and priest of the home after his father's death
2. Chief of chosen family and heir of promised family
3. Able to invoke the blessings of Abraham

    And give you the blessing of Abraham, to you and your descendants with you, that you may inherit the land. In which you are a stranger, which God gave to Abraham." (Genesis 28:4)

The New Testament adds a most troubling commentary in Romans 9:12-13:

> *It was said to her, "The older shall serve the younger." As it is written, "Jacob I have loved, but Esau I have hated.*

Before we go overboard thinking that the cards were stacked against Esau, we must note that his life was full of bad choices. At a weak moment, he profaned the sacred by taking the physical and spiritual benefit of the firstborn and selling it to his brother for a bowl of food.

When it came time for the blessing to be passed down from Dad, preparations were made for Esau to kill a deer and make some special stew for his father to eat. Jacob got wind of the deal, mom helped him make some substitute stew, and Jacob got there first. Father Isaac fell for the deception and Esau was robbed of the blessing.

It is no surprise that the Bible reveals that Esau hated his brother Jacob and immediately began to plan his death. (Genesis 27:4) To remedy the situation, Jacob decided to head toward his Uncle Laban's house to allow Esau some time to cool off and get over the whole ordeal. He did not realize that it would be years before they would see each other again.

In the Bible, the focus of the story shifts to Jacob's life in the land of Haran and not much is revealed about Esau. We know he married someone of whom his parents did not approve (Genesis 28:8-9), and through time became quite prosperous in a land called Edom. Beyond that, we are in the dark until Jacob decided to return home and was scared to death at the prospect of coming face to face with Esau. After all, at their last meeting, Esau had threatened Jacob's life.

Imagine how startled Jacob was at the meeting when Esau greeted him with tears, hugs, and kisses! (Genesis 33) What had happened in those intervening years to create such a change? On the surface it appears a notable miracle of the Lord, but Genesis 33:9 gives a clearer insight. Esau had enough material wealth to be satisfied in life and this was all that really mattered to him. It had nothing to do with spiritual transformation in his life, or even regret that he had lost the right of the firstborn to his brother.

In this example, we see a faulty and unhealthy way to deal with the past. It rejects forgiveness and repentance as the pathway to healing and instead embraces the philosophy that states, "Just get over it and move on with your life." In outward appearance, everything seems normal and the problem seems to be gone. However, there is something beneath the surface that is costing the person big-time.

> *Looking carefully lest anyone fall short of the grace of God; lest any root of bitterness springing up cause trouble, and by this many become defiled; [16] lest there be any fornicator or profane person like Esau, who for one morsel of food sold his birthright. (Hebrews 12:15-16)*

It is possible to have a root of bitterness in one's life that is undetected but still impacts a person spiritually and at times emotionally. The word *defiled* means to dye with color or stain. Most of us have had the experience where a red sock accidentally got placed in a washing machine full of white clothes. Everything comes out with a pink hue because the sock has tainted the entire load of clothes. For Esau this meant moving on with his life and living for the present world, rather than pursuing a joyous relationship with God.

In the same manner, an experience from the past can taint our lives and cause us to miss out on valuable spiritual blessings and emotional well-being. We press on with our life and become convinced that it does not even affect us any longer. We may become defensive when anyone suggests the possibility that we are bothered by the past issue or the person who caused the problem. It is simply easier to declare, "That happened a long time ago, and I am over it."

> *Example-Joe was a man who genuinely loved the Lord and willingly served with passion in the local church. The problem was that he seemed to regularly move from church to church after a period of time. Each time the reason for leaving would be related to changes in the church. He could not agree with the dress standards, music, or some other related topic. In every case, he would attempt to put the past behind him and start all over in a new church.*
>
> *Without fail, he would sense his new pastor heading in the same direction that took place in his former church. He would begin by approaching the pastor to question what was going on and gently expressing his disapproval, while the pastor would attempt to reassure him of his desire to follow the Lord's leading. In time, more and more situations would trouble him, and he would pray for the Lord to re-direct the church leadership. He would seek to stay on because he loved his Sunday School class and did not want to leave the church fellowship. Eventually he would leave and the whole process would begin again.*
>
> *What Joe failed to realize was that early on he had been hurt by an abusive church leader, and without realizing it he believed that all church leaders were of the same ilk. Because he had failed to respond God's way, his future authority always seemed to develop problems*

> *that caused him to move on to another place. Unfortunately, he did not realize that he had a problem being under authority. By making changes based on the belief that he was "just doing what was right," it allowed him to avoid God-given authority in his life.*
>
> *No one who knew Joe would ever believe he struggled with authority. He was careful not to speak bad about church leadership, and he sought to lead an exemplary life that would remove any doubt that he was right in leaving a church. Unfortunately, this cost Joe the ability to build life-long friendships and hindered his effectiveness in the Lord's work - not to mention that he would experience a martyr's complex, because he felt he had to leave another church because of his convictions. The church would also suffer for a while because they had grown to love him.*

Impotent man: I must accept my condition

> *When Jesus saw him lying there, and knew that he already had been in that condition a long time, He said to him, "Do you want to be made well?" The sick man answered Him, "Sir, I have no man to put me into the pool when the water is stirred up; but while I am coming, another steps down before me." (John 5:6-7)*

This is a notable miracle as Jesus caused a man to walk who for thirty-eight years had been in a deplorable condition. We must acknowledge the faith of the man who upon the simple command of Christ, got up and began to walk. However, I am convinced there are some telling signs that may lead us to find some unhealthy problems in his answer.

It is important to note that his answer in verse seven had nothing to do with the question. I know there were hindrances to be overcome, but Jesus was not asking if he could be healed, but rather if he *wanted* to be healed. In fairness to the man's response, he was looking at the pool of water as a means to bring healing instead of Jesus which may have led to the answer. Still, we may need to take a moment to read between the lines.

Anyone who has been stuck with the same problem for years can relate to the man's negative attitude. Lying on the ground and depending on others to get from place to place would be very annoying and we should not make light of the man's despair. However, there are some things about his answer that lead us to believe his past was affecting his present.

1. *Vulnerability* - I am all alone here and in a condition that requires someone else to help. This is not of my choosing and I never seem to catch a break. There is always someone else who gets the jump on me, and I am stuck with no solution.

2. *Excuses* - I am doing the best I can by being here and heading in the right direction when the water moves. There is no way I am ever going to be fast enough to be first.

3. *Rejection syndrome* - Nobody is willing to help me. Everyone else has their own problems, and I do not even have a friend who can stay down here to assist me.

4. *Self-pity* - Any person with compassion would be in tears if he was there and personally heard this man's answer. He would probably even want to make a contribution to help him be healed. You cannot read the answer without feeling his pain.

It would seem that this man had grown accustomed to his lot in life and probably felt he would always be unable to walk. He had accepted his past and decided to live with it. However, that did not stop him from wallowing in a sense of despair at his hopeless condition. We would not want to attack a lame man, but his negative attitude does stand out.

Note that Jesus did not stop to consider his objections. He was about to show this man His power, and the man would never be the same. Christ's desire was to deliver the man from the bondage of the past, not to accept his problem and allow him to wallow in self-pity.

Example-An elderly woman came for counsel who was past functioning because of an anxiety attack. She was convinced she was a believer in Jesus Christ, but admitted she had not been active in the Word or as faithful to church as she should have been. At times she would break into tears, and at other times in her life, she could function quite normally.

As is often the case, she had received a good bit of information from other professionals and friends. She related that she had a chemical imbalance in the brain, and the medication helped but never completely cured her of her problem. She noted that she had inherited part of the problem from her mother. She could readily remember her mother at a certain age having a nervous breakdown and thinking that she would probably one day have the same thing happen to her.

Whenever I would confront any argument with something the Bible says, her response would be, "But they say" or "the doctor says" and would directly refute what the Scripture said. After a while, she thanked me for spending time with her since her pastor would not, and then she prepared to leave. I gave her a few Scriptures on which to meditate with the conviction they would help, but they probably would not in her case since she would not use them. It was easier for her to believe that she was destined to be anxious rather than take the steps of faith to overcome.

Samson: I must take care of myself

No doubt, Samson is the best known of all the judges. A free spirit, who killed lions with his bare hands and who single-handedly was able to overcome a thousand enemies, has a natural appeal that would demand hero worship. Children are spellbound when told of his heroic physical strength, but sadly he stands out as a dismal moral failure. His life is a testimony to the failure of a person to reach his potential, and the amazing way God chooses to use weak people.

Samson made a poor choice early in his life that caused long-term pain and led him to adopt a self-serving lifestyle. It began with a powerful attraction to a Philistine woman that he just could not live without, despite the fact that the Philistines were the sworn enemies of Samson's nation. His parents' attempt to dissuade him from a Philistine wife made him more determined to marry her.

A strange thing happened after the wedding. His bride was threatened by the town's people if she did not uncover the answer to a riddle Samson had used to make a wager with them. Her seduction of her husband worked because he revealed the answer. The town's people won the bet, and Samson executed revenge for his loss. In his absence, his wife was given to someone else to marry after a period of time. Truth is stranger than fiction.

Samson's behavior after this strange turn of events left him bitter and with a constant desire to take matters into his own hands. Most notable was his desire to get even as he unleashed foxes with firebrands into the harvest fields of the Philistines and then sought to wipe them out with only a donkey's jawbone as a weapon. Hurt drives a person to get even, never really knowing what even is.

There are two things in Samson's life that stand out as characteristics of the person who decides that hurt means learning to take care of one's self. The first characteristic is that passion rules decision making; in fact, it seems that everything one does is "me"-centered. Samson had a life full of such examples:

- He chose a wife because she pleased him.

  Then he went down and talked with the woman; and she pleased Samson well. (Judges 14:7)

- He wreaked havoc in the corn fields of the Philistines to vindicate himself and waged war in order to avenge himself.

  Samson said to them, "Since you would do a thing like this, I will surely take revenge on you, and after that I will cease." (Judges 15:7)

- The only time we see him calling on the Lord was when he was thirsty and needed to be satisfied.

  Then he became very thirsty; so he cried out to the LORD and said, "You have given this great deliverance by the hand of Your servant; and now shall I die of thirst and fall into the hand of the uncircumcised?"(Judges 15:18)

- He protected himself emotionally after a failed marriage by choosing a prostitute for companionship.

  Now Samson went to Gaza and saw a harlot there, and went in to her. (Judges 16:1)

- Despite three warning signs of betrayal by Delilah (Judges 16:9, 12, 14), he enjoyed the illicit relationship too much to give her up.

  Now men were lying in wait, staying with her in the room. And she said to him, "The Philistines are upon you, Samson!" But he broke the bowstrings as a strand of yarn breaks when it touches fire. So the secret of his strength was not known. (Judges 16:9)

> *Therefore Delilah took new ropes and bound him with them, and said to him, "The Philistines are upon you, Samson!" And men were lying in wait, staying in the room. But he broke them off his arms like a thread. (Judges 16:12)*
>
> *So she wove it tightly with the batten of the loom, and said to him, "The Philistines are upon you, Samson!" But he awoke from his sleep, and pulled out the batten and the web from the loom. (Judges 16:14)*

The other major sign of an "I must take care of me" attitude is the artful skill of manipulation. Samson manipulated his parents by insisting on a wife and deceived them about his disobedience to the law by eating honey from the carcass of the lion. (Judges 14:9) He played the manipulation game with Delilah about the secret of his strength on three separate occasions before he actually divulged the truth. It is ironic that he was outwitted by the manipulation of Delilah.

The sad life of Samson's self-centeredness ended in tragedy beyond description. We find him the object of the Philistines ridicule, with his eyes put out and living out his life in slavery. Even his last great feat of strength, which destroyed more enemies at one time than in his entire life, is marred by his own selfish motives.

> *"O Lord God, remember me, I pray thee, only this once, O God, that I may be at once avenged of the Philistines for my two eyes". – Samson*
>
> *Then Samson called to the LORD, saying, "O Lord GOD, remember me, I pray! Strengthen me, I pray, just this once, O God, that I may with one blow take vengeance on the Philistines for my two eyes!" Judges 16:28*
>
> E*xample-Natalie hoped to shock the counselor with the revelation that she was risking her marriage and endangering her life with multiple affairs that often involved men she barely knew. She could not comprehend her behavior since she had given her life to Christ years previously and had often repented of her actions only to repeat the transgression. She was caught in a desperate cycle of failure and saw little hope of overcoming.*

In time it was revealed that she had been abused by a sibling, and her mother either did not believe her, or worse, chose not to protect her. Her mother had long passed from this life, but Natalie was still filled with hatred and unresolved questions of how a mother could be so cruel. Eventually she would be able to release her mother from the debt she was owed in an undeserved act of forgiveness.

I share her story because she had turned to a self-absorbed life to cover her pain. What stands out was the way Natalie hid any emotions, and determined to not let another human being hurt her. Her relationship with her husband was matter-of-fact and left no room for intimacy. People who came across her path knew she would not open up and really allow them into her world.

Natalie's life was driven by her determination to be in charge and to not take anything from anyone. Even her affairs that contained some of the typical motives of being close to someone or the thrill of illicit sex was overshadowed by one other factor. Natalie was in control. The bottom line was that Natalie had to protect herself because she could not trust anyone else.

Absalom: I must get even

In the first three ways people attempt to get over their pasts, we often falsely conclude that these are legitimate ways and even condone such behavior. Not much damage is done to us if others seek to get over the past by just moving on with their lives, accepting undesirable present conditions, or even if they choose to live a cold, calculating self-centered life. Not everyone is cut out to deal with the past by such tranquil solutions. It seems more productive to roll up the sleeves and try to get even.

Enter Absalom. Absalom was a king's son born with the silver spoon in his mouth and endowed with traits that would make the average person jealous. Endowed with extremely good looks, a way with words, and people skills, it would seem that he had it all. An unfortunate event created a bitter spot in his heart that would ultimately lead to his destruction.

Absalom had a beautiful sister who was raped by a step-brother, Amnon. For two years Absalom harbored revenge in his heart, and at the opportune time, he took Amnon's life. Most would conclude that the matter was settled, and assume Absalom would get over the past. On the surface that would seem true since after a period of time, he was reconciled to his father, King David, and resumed what most would think was a normal life.

Herein is the faulty assumption of the nature of revenge. As a person is plotting against the one who has wronged him, he assumes that all will be over once he gets even. Absalom is proof that such is not the case and that the revenge only opens the person's life up to even more treacherous behavior. Revenge is always proof of rebellion in the heart because a person is unwilling to allow God to meet out justice to those who have done them a disservice.

In time, Absalom rebelled against his father who loved him deeply and treated him with nothing but fairness and mercy. His life was cut short in military conflict, and he left behind a trail of betrayal and misery for the few who loved him. Whoever concludes that revenge is sweet is definitely mistaken.

> *Example-Who was to blame for Karen and Steve's marriage coming to the point of divorce was hard to decide. In time it would become evident that both she and her husband had been traveling a rocky road for quite some time, and both would become involved in illicit relationships. For years, they had hidden their unhappiness with busy lifestyles and lots of involvement in the church. Despite counseling, it became evident that the marriage was over.*
>
> *For Karen the old adages were true, "I cannot live with you and I cannot live without you," and "Since I cannot have you, neither can anyone else." She made it her goal in life to make Steve's life miserable. Outbursts of anger caused the children to hate him, and even false accusations to the police in order to have her husband arrested were all a part of a scheme to get even. A person could not be in her presence long before she was railing on her husband. Nothing seemed to appease her wrath.*
>
> *In the Lord's mercy, He eventually brought Karen to the end of herself and released her from her bitterness. She was shaken to reality when she was standing before a judge who threatened to leave her in jail if she failed to stop her tactics of seeking to get even with her ex-husband. Only the Lord knows for sure if her heart was released from the bondage of desiring revenge, but she at least avoided taking Absalom's route of murder.*

Compare the four unhealthy ways to get over the past:

Reasoning (mind)	**Result (heart)**	**Reaction (flesh)**
I must get over it	self-centered	affected his values
I must accept my condition	self-pity	made him a victim
I must take care of myself	self-indulgent	led to vice
I must get even	self-gratification	made him vengeful

This is honestly where many Christians get stuck in their spiritual progress. The soul is bogged down in a mire of why, what if's and a sense that life is not fair. There must be a solution applied before the journey to soul prosperity can proceed.

MY SOUL MUST FIND FORGIVENESS

"Out, damned spot! Out, I say!" This has become one of the most famous quotes in literary history uttered by Lady Macbeth as she dream-walked in the corridors of the castle attempting to rub the blood stains from her hands. Guilt had consumed her life since she assisted her husband in the ghastly murders of Duncan and his servants. Yet nothing would relieve her tortured conscience.

We all have a past, and to a greater or lesser degree, it attempts to affect our present. Satan sees to that. It is often puzzling that the new birth signals a fresh start and at the point we experience salvation, starting over seems to be a reality. Quickly though, the new wears off and often the soul is mired in confusing chains from the past. The past binds us in two primary ways:

- By attempting to control you with guilt for what you have done in the past.
- By attempting to frustrate you with the things that happened to you in the past.

As a young person I remember sitting in a service when an elderly lady began to sing a special.

> "Oh you can't do wrong and get by,
>
> No matter how hard you may try,
>
> So just do what you please, and try to feel at ease,
>
> For you can't do wrong and get by."

Humans may disagree fervently about what constitutes right and wrong behavior, but it is an accepted norm that God will punish those who do wrong. It satisfies our sense of justice. Even for the Christian, who understands the love of God that led Him to punish His Son for his sins, he is often reminded that he must suffer consequences for his past actions. This becomes a two-edged sword when the mind is not only convinced that he must be punished for his past, but also that God cannot bless him in the present because of his past.

Emotionally, a person can become handicapped in the way they process the feelings of guilt over past behavior. Some become trapped in feelings of inadequacy and become convinced they will never be able to change their behavior. Others take a different path of being driven to earn God's favor by living a better life and performing to make up for the past.

It is at this point that the flesh kicks in to solve the problem through a vicious cycle that some Christians seem to remain in for a lifetime. There is an incident in the life of Peter that clearly demonstrates this cycle where he met with colossal failure and actually denied the Lord. (Mark 14) Most of us will be able to see ourselves in Peter's failure.

Dependent on my own strength - Mark 14:29, 31

Peter was insulted by the Lord's remark that all the disciples would fail so he angrily let it be known that he would never do such a thing. Reliance on self is always rooted in pride; pride is an enemy of God's grace. It starts with an attitude that somehow I am different than everyone else and there are certain things I could never do. One thing for certain is that every Christian is capable of any sin or failure. In fact, when the Christian protests loudly about a particular transgression or is very judgmental of another believer who has failed in that area it can lead to his own downfall. (Galatians 6:1)

Peter had the best intentions, but he misread his own heart and miscalculated what he would do when the pressure was on. Try to imagine his spirit revealed in verse 31 when he protested more loudly against the Lord *who already knew what was going to take place.* That moment in time is when Peter's real failure occurred as his arrogance took over and he set out to prove Jesus wrong about his prediction.

My effort to succeed – Mark 14:47

John's Gospel (18:10) reveals that the zealot servant referred to in Mark 14:47 was none other than Peter himself. He was determined to keep his promise to die rather than to forsake Christ in His time of distress so with a sword he took matters into his own hands. The irony is that he was standing in the way of Christ going to the cross by taking matters into his own hands. This trap of self-effort is set when someone has made a vow to love Christ and do His will so he redoubles his efforts to be faithful to that promise.

This problem of self-determination can be so confusing because most people have been taught that God will bless our efforts to serve Him. For most of the Christian life our advisors have told us when we were struggling spiritually to just pray more, study the Bible more, go to church more and things will get better. Such challenges cause most people's pride to kick in and they set off to redouble their efforts to do more for Christ. Those attempts will always fail because God abhors our strength since it interferes with His power to work through His people.

Drifting away from Christ – Mark 14:54

Peter's physical proximity to Christ as he warms himself at the enemies' fire is a reflection of the spiritual condition of a Christian when he attempts to live the Christian life under his own power. I am not suggesting that Christ withdraws from us, but instead we are removing ourselves from a life of faith in receiving His influence. As we distance ourselves, we lose our joy of fellowship and the power of Christ against trials and temptations. In Peter's case, we find him drawing closer to the enemies of Christ and participating in behavior that is out of character with whom he really was.

Nothing is more disturbing than watching Christians who have experienced life in Christ drift aimlessly back to a life of defeat. Some stray to places where their behavior does not match the confession of faith in Christ, while others isolate themselves from Christian fellowship as they wrestle with guilt and a feeling of helplessness to return to the previous level of faith. Some even question whether they were truly converted to Christ.

Failure – Mark 14:68, 71

Does it seem strange to you that a person, who just a few hours before professed willingness to die and took out a sword to prove his point, is now *cursing and denying* Jesus Christ? Never underestimate the fickleness of human nature dominated by the flesh. Vows are quickly forgotten and the person can find themselves in the most awkward positions which they never dreamed could happen.

I am reminded of a time when as a teenager I was controlled by behavior which was contrary to my testimony of being a believer in Christ. A few of my friends and I along with my little brother took the family car down to the local elementary school to play baseball. I parked the car on the right side of the highway and we all, except for my little brother, proceeded to cross the road to the ball field. To my horror I watched as a driver came around the curve, lost control of his car, and collided with my parked car. My little brother was pinned between the two cars.

Convinced he was going to die, I began to cry out to the Lord and make promises that if He would spare my brother's life I would live for Him and do His will no matter what. To my amazement my brother had only bruises and one laceration; the hospital released him that same day. Even years later I am astounded how the weight of those two cars crashing together did not crush my brother to death or at least break a number of bones.

Did I live up to my end of the vow? Of course not. That night when the crisis was over, I was back with my friends participating in the same sins I had been doing. I am just one example of a myriad of Christians across the body of Christ who has failed the Lord and it is extremely ugly and devastating. Ministers who are destroyed by immorality, homes wrecked by divorce, lives enslaved by destructive habits, and an endless litany of lives who experience failure by relying on self in place of relying on the influence of the Holy Spirit.

Frustration – Mark 14:72

It is not difficult to visualize Peter's brokenness at that point when he realized his failure or to relate to him through our own experiences. Far too many individuals have been in my office sobbing because the destructive force of sin has ruined their life. I have experienced more than a few of those times when the offence of a transgression has come crushing down on me like a weightlifter who has attempted to lift too much on the bench press. It is a misery that is indescribable and leaves a person questioning his relationship with God and convinces him the Lord will never trust him again.

Some may attempt to quit and go back to living as they did in the pre-Christ days. In my opinion that is the route Peter took in John 21:3. It is exciting to know the Lord will not allow us to stay stuck in this cycle of failure, but as he did with Peter, confront us with inspection, grant to us pardon, and set us back on the right course.

Cycle of Failure
Mark 14

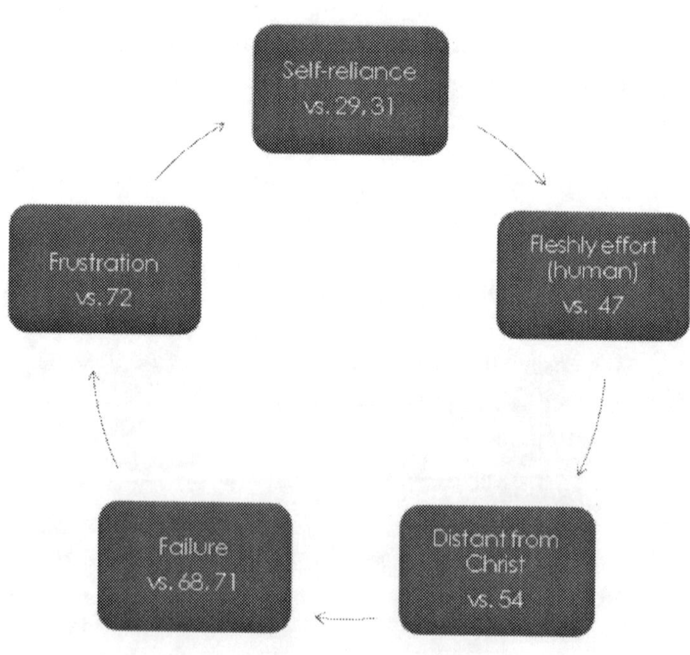

The answer is forgiveness. You must accept that God knows your past and chooses to forgive you through His Son. Before you begin with your logical arguments, stop and understand that there is no other way off this highway of frustration and failure. If you are saying, "I already knew that," please understand that knowing the facts of forgiveness is not the same as *experiencing* forgiveness and the assurance that everything is all right with God.

- Remorse-I am troubled by my behavior and face my guilt.

  Key word: **Confused** (II Corinthians 7:9-10) Why did I do it? What will it cost? I am experiencing regret over the action.

- Repent-I want life change, recognize I am powerless to change myself, and turn to God for change.

  Key word: **Confess** (I John 1:9) "Confession in its truest sense involves despising the sin, being grieved by it, and judging it." John McArthur

- Removal-I come to understand my sin is gone.

  Key word: **Convinced** (Colossians 2:14) By faith I receive the finished work of Christ.

- Righteousness-I am made right through Christ

  Key word: **Claim** (Hebrews 11:4, I Corinthians 1:30) All my acceptance is based on Christ, not my works.

Forgiveness is received when you come to the end of your human effort. When you stop wallowing in self-pity, throw yourself fully on the righteousness of Jesus Christ, and realize you will never be worthy of forgiveness, you will then find that God is willing to forgive. It defies human reasoning, but forgiveness opens the prison door from your guilt of the past.

FORGIVEN SOULS FORGIVE

It is one thing to be forgiven; it is another thing to be able to forgive. I remind you that Satan tries to trap us by holding us in guilt for our past behavior, but he also attempts to enslave believers in the prison of an unforgiving spirit. The latter seems to be his most effective tool in hindering spiritual progress in the life of a believer, by blinding the person from the personal destruction that takes place in the unforgiving heart.

Bruce and Mary sat in my office after they had visited our church about a dozen times. After exchanging a few pleasantries about how the church was ministering to them, Mary began to cry. "We have not been in church for 16 years and we did not know what we were missing. I know this is no excuse but..."

The story that unfolded touched my heart and I cried with this couple. They had a severely retarded little girl who, as a teenager, was put in a group home for part of each week so she could be taken care of, and they could maintain a semi-normal life for the rest of the family. One night, through the neglect of one of the workers, their daughter was severely burned while bathing. She suffered in the hospital for 28 days before she died. Through tears Mary said, "I know I need to forgive this worker, but I do not know if I can."

Looking back over 30 years of counseling has caused me to see that the majority of people with whom I have dealt had their problems severely complicated by the frustration of an unforgiving spirit. Not all of them could see the direct connection between what they were going through in the present and how something that happened years ago could be hindering the freedom of their soul. When the Lord first began to show me this correlation, it drove me to the Scriptures for answers.

On one occasion, Jesus was instructing his disciples on what to do when someone wronged them. As was often the case, the teaching ended with a question-and-answer time in which the disciples were seeking clarification, or perhaps seeking to justify their own spirituality by showing how willing they were to apply the teaching. In a magnanimous gesture Peter asks, "How often should I forgive my brother, seven times?" Most likely he thought the number was a little high, but Peter wanted to flaunt his great spirituality.

Imagine the shock of Jesus' answer. "Not seven times, but until seven times seventy." Now in his masterful way, Jesus began to explain himself in story form. It is a story to which the common person can relate with unnamed people described in ways that drive home the issue and underscore the imperative of forgiveness.

> *Then Peter came to Him and said, "Lord, how often shall my brother sin against me, and I forgive him? Up to seven times?" Jesus said to him, "I do not say to you, up to seven times, but up to seventy times seven. Therefore the kingdom of heaven is like a certain king who wanted to settle accounts with his servants. And when he had begun to settle accounts, one was brought to him who owed him ten thousand talents. But as he was not able to pay, his master commanded that he be sold, with his wife and children and all that he had, and that payment be made. The servant therefore fell down before him, saying, 'Master, have patience with me, and I will pay you all.' Then the master of that servant was moved with compassion, released him, and forgave him the debt. "But that servant went out and found one of his fellow servants who owed him a hundred denarii; and he laid hands on him and took him by the throat, saying, 'Pay me what you owe!' So his fellow servant fell down at his feet and begged him, saying, 'Have patience with me, and I will pay you all.' And he would not, but went and threw him into prison till he should pay the debt. So when his fellow servants saw what had been done, they were very grieved, and came and told their master all that had been done. Then his master, after he had called him, said to him, 'You wicked servant! I forgave you all that debt because you begged me. Should you not also have had compassion on your fellow servant, just as I had pity on you?' And his master was angry, and delivered him to the torturers until he should pay all that was due to him. "So My heavenly Father also will do*

> *to you if each of you, from his heart, does not forgive his brother his trespasses."(Matthew 18:21-35)*

The first debtor in the story owed his king, by today's standard, millions of dollars. Justice of the law demanded he and his family be put into debtor prison until full payment was received. In humility, he begged for leniency and vowed he would pay the debt in full. Everyone present, including the king, knew the servant was incapable of fulfilling the promise, but with a gracious act of forgiveness, the king releases the servant.

The story takes an ugly turn downward as the servant went out to find someone who owed him a paltry sum of money. When the man was unable to pay he threw him into prison! The king's reaction gives us insight into the high cost of not forgiving. What does it mean to "deliver him to the torturers," seeing the application Jesus made in verse 35?

In reality, human forgiveness is more for the person ***granting*** forgiveness than it is for the one ***receiving***. Often, the ones who harm us either do not realize what they have done, or they feel justified in their actions, or, in some cases, they know the pain but could care less. Many walk away from those wrongs and soon forget the incident while the victim may languish for years with continuing distress.

It is impossible to gauge the degree of problems that result from an unforgiving spirit, but, for those who have dealt with these issues, it is safe to say it is ***torture***. Spiritually, the individual is robbed of a joyous relationship with God and is plagued by feelings of guilt.

> *"And whenever you stand praying, if you have anything against anyone, forgive him, that your Father in heaven may also forgive you your trespasses. But if you do not forgive, neither will your Father in heaven forgive your trespasses." (Mark 11:25-26)*

Emotionally, the person is racked with fear, anger, revenge, bitterness and other unhealthy emotions every time he consciously or unconsciously remembers the wrong. This spiritual and emotional torture wreaks havoc on the human body, bringing damage to vital organs and stress that can cause other physical ailments.

A seven year study of 2,100 men revealed that "unforgiving thoughts prompted more aversive emotion and significantly higher forehead muscle tension, skin conductance, heart rate, and blood pressure changes over the base line." These physiological changes persisted even after the participants stopped remembering the hurtful events. (www.internalfocus.com)

Before we look at the benefit of forgiveness, it may be wise to explore some common misconceptions about forgiveness.

1. I do not need to forgive because the person is not sorry for what he did.

   This indicates the person must meet certain requirements to deserve forgiveness. The truth is forgiveness is always undeserved and is a result of grace.

   > *In Him we have redemption through His blood, the forgiveness of sins, according to the riches of His grace. (Ephesians 1:7)*

In Jesus' example of forgiving seven times seventy, you would tend to question the sincerity of the person's continual repentance.

2. By forgiving, I am excusing the wrongdoer's behavior.

   You are not forgiving the behavior, but are releasing the person from the debt of how that behavior affected you. Forgiveness releases you from reliving the wrong over and over again in your mind along with accompanying thoughts of revenge. It allows you to cease attacking the offender to other people through gossip and evil speaking.

3. The person I forgive is now released from the consequences of his wrong.

   Even though you forgive your offender, there may be consequences for the wrong committed. An abuse victim can forgive her attacker and still expect law enforcement to arrest and prosecute him. Forgiveness removes revenge from your heart and your right to judge, but it does not ignore justice. In the same realm, you may forgive a person for the way his sin affects you, but he will still one day give an account for that transgression before God.

4. Forgive and forget.

Hebrews 10:17 "And their sins and iniquities I will remember no more." One of the things we believe about God is that He is all-knowing. It is our contention that God is perfect in His thinking and is unable to forget. When He forgives our sin, He chooses not to remember them anymore. When you forgive someone, Satan is a master at bringing the offense up in your mind and tormenting you with the injustice that the wrongdoer has not been punished. You would never be able to forget, but you can choose not to remember because you have released the person from the debt.

5. Now that I have forgiven, I want our relationship to be restored.

   When trust is betrayed, simply going back to the way things were may not be wise. You do not have to be best friends now that forgiveness has taken place, and being around that person may be uncomfortable. However, you are expected to show genuine love, and sometimes love can take place at a distance.

   > *And Samuel went no more to see Saul until the day of his death. Nevertheless Samuel mourned for Saul, and the LORD regretted that He had made Saul king over Israel. (1 Samuel 15:35)*

In this Biblical example, Samuel never lost his love for King Saul, but Saul's behavior prevented them from continuing a relationship.

6. I am over that, so I must have forgiven the person.

   Time has a way of healing our hurts, but that is not proof of forgiveness. If you truly forgive, most likely you will remember when that took place because it created a breakthrough in your heart. Certain people have an easier time moving on with their lives, but if forgiveness has not taken place, there will be complications.

A friend of mine struggled for years with his relationship to his father. While he was very young, his dad chose a lifestyle of chasing women and partying over his family. As a teen, my friend came to know Christ but it did not replace the void his absent father left. He was constantly finding himself with the desire for his dad to return and make his transgression against him right. Finally, in desperation he decided to forgive his dad.

He decided to go in person to speak with him. At the meeting, he attempted to share how the things his dad had done had hurt him deeply. He was very respectful, and in a very emotional moment, told his dad he forgave him. He waited for his response. Imagine the wave of anger that struck when his dad replied, "I did not really do anything to you."

This brings us to an important point that Jesus illustrated in the Gospels. There is a contrast draw between the person who has offended someone and the person who is offended and it is illustrated by Jesus in describing two people at worship. In Matthew 5:23-24, the author makes it clear that if I come to worship God and know someone has something against me, I am to immediately leave the altar and go seek my friend's forgiveness.

> *Therefore if you bring your gift to the altar, and there remember that your brother has something against you, leave your gift there before the altar, and go your way. First be reconciled to your brother, and then come and offer your gift (Matthew 5:23-24)*

On the other hand, if I am at worship and remember I have been wronged by my brother, I must forgive.

> *"And whenever you stand praying, if you have anything against anyone, forgive him, that your Father in heaven may also forgive you your trespasses. (Mark 11:25)*

In the first case, the implication is that I must not continue to worship until I have gone to my brother to seek his forgiveness. In the other example, it is not necessary to go to the person or for them to acknowledge the need to be forgiven. This protects us from many harmful complications in the matter of forgiveness.

The Blessing of Forgiveness

Forgiveness is to the soul what Drano is to the plumbing in your house. When you fail to forgive, you begin to relive past events over and over in your mind and may even choose imaginary responses to what could have been done differently. Those haunting memories create anguish and often taint your present relationships with the important people in your life. At times, you may create a fantasy world that dreams of that Walton's Mountain moment when the person who wronged you comes to apologize and beg for forgiveness. You may think, "I know they are going to wake up to the grief they have caused in my life."

Would it not be nice to get out of the debt collection business? I can think of no worse way to make a living than to try to chase down people who are unable to pay what they owe and then twist their arm to get it out of them. Yet time and time again I speak with people who say, "I cannot forgive them for what they did to me." So they are determined to collect even if it drains a little out of their own soul each day.

It is vital to comprehend that forgiveness is a choice, not a feeling. If Satan can keep a person under the impression he must wait until he feels forgiveness or that he is not able to forgive, the trap is set. That person will continue to be eaten up by the consequences of an unforgiving spirit not realizing it is hurting himself more than it is the person who committed the transgression.

Understand that forgiving is a divine trait not well distributed by earthlings. So, God gives us a sure-fire way to forgive.

> *And be kind to one another, tenderhearted, forgiving one another, even as God in Christ forgave you. (Ephesians 4:32)*

It is never pleasant for us to admit that what someone has done to me could never be as bad as what I have done to God. When you did not deserve forgiveness because of the multitude of your wrongs against God, He chose to release you from the debt through His Son, Jesus Christ. Whatever the other person owes you is paltry compared to what you have done to God in your choice of sin and your rejection of Him. So God's grace is sufficient for you to say, "I forgive you." Remember this is vital if you are to experience your soul being set free to enjoy what the Lord intended for his people.

TRUTH OR CONSEQUENCES IN THE SOUL

Receiving and granting forgiveness releases the individual from a huge weight of guilt that has affected thinking and feelings. Momentarily it may give a sense of complete wholeness to the soul and the person may be deceived into thinking the battle is over and he is fixed. In truth, forgiveness has only cleared the path so that he can pursue soul prosperity as God intended. As is always the case, this pursuit begins in the depository of the mind.

Before a person knows Christ, the mind is the beginning path to our quest for God. Unfortunately, it is also the place where our journey away from God starts. There is a perfect illustration of this in the Old Testament when God wanted to confront Israel with the absurdity of idols, so He used the prophet Isaiah to describe a man who found a piece of wood and made himself a fire. From the fire he warmed himself, cooked a meal of meat and bread, and afterward, took the leftover wood and concluded that this wood which had warmed his body and filled his belly was worthy of worship. In blindness, he carved an idol and bowed down to pay homage not recognizing the foolishness of his own actions. After the fire was out, he was once again hungry and there was nothing left to feed on but ashes. It finally registered and he declared, "Is there not a lie in my right hand?" (Isaiah 44:20)

The modern mind scoffs at this ridiculous sight of a man worshipping a tree. We prefer more extravagant gods of wealth, sports, fame, power, and an endless array of enticing myths that capture our affection. We have replaced idols of wood with thousands of other things that we think will satisfy the soul, but always end with the same conclusion: It is a lie. Still, with wide-eyed enthusiasm, we press on with resolve that around the next corner we will find the one thing that will fill the hole in my heart.

Humanity may marvel at the superior intellect of certain people, but God does not have much good to say about the mind of the person outside of Christ.

> *This I say, therefore, and testify in the Lord, that you should no longer walk as the rest ofthe Gentiles walk, in the futility of their mind, having their understanding darkened, being alienated from the life of God, because of the ignorance that is in them, because of the blindness of their heart; who, being past feeling, have given themselves over to lewdness, to work all uncleanness with greediness. But you have not so learned Christ.(Ephesians 4:17-20)*

The mind is hopelessly confused and closed to the things of God. Ignorance has made them indifferent to life that is available from God in Jesus Christ, and they continue on as though they will solve life's problems by their wisdom. Paul then turned to the Christians to let them know that was not the case for those who know Christ. For them, the mind had been reconciled (Colossians 1:21) and now needs to be transformed. (Romans 12:2)

> *And you, who once were alienated and enemies in your mind by wicked works, yet now He has reconciled. (Colossians 1:21)*

> *And do not be conformed to this world, but be transformed by the renewing of your mind, that you may prove what is that good and acceptable and perfect will of God. (Romans 12:2)*

The only objective of the mind that is worth achieving is to know God.

> *'But let him who glories glory in this, That he understands and knows Me,*

> *That I am the LORD, exercising lovingkindness, judgment, and righteousness in the earth. For in these I delight,' says the LORD. (Jeremiah 9:24)*

> *And this is eternal life, that they may know You, the only true God, and Jesus Christ whom You have sent. (John 17:3)*

This pursuit is not just knowing facts about God like the things we learned as children in Sunday School, but experiencing God in a real and vital relationship. It is coming to understand His ways and plans, and feeling His desires. This happens when you begin to walk with God in his word so that you begin thinking His thoughts, and are able to comprehend His great nature, which is the pursuit of the transformed mind.

Examine how this takes place. God reveals that Jesus is the Truth (John 14:6) and His Word is Truth. (John 17:17)

> *Jesus said to him, "I am the way, the truth, and the life. No one comes to the Father except through Me. (John 14:6)*

> *Sanctify them by Your truth. Your word is truth. (John 17:17)*

No small wonder that the new Christian suddenly has a thirst for that truth (I Peter 2:2), and begins a lifelong journey to discover and apply truth to his life.

> *As newborn babes, desire the pure milk of the word, that you may grow thereby. (1 Peter 2:2)*

The Guide is the Holy Spirit (John 16:13), who is the only One able to make sure he stays on the path of truth and does not veer off of the course.

> *However, when He, the Spirit of truth, has come, He will guide you into all truth; for He will not speak on His own authority, but whatever He hears He will speak; and He will tell you things to come. (John 16:13)*

The temptation is to believe that, because the Holy Spirit resides in the Christian, the battle for the mind is over, when in fact, this is where Satan does his greatest work. In both subtle and direct ways attacks are made upon the mind by promoting error. Jesus said, "You will know the truth, and the truth will set you free" (John 8:32), then rest assured lies and half-truths will be promoted by Jesus' enemy to keep people in bondage. All too often many believers are unable to discern the difference between truth and error.

This is why in every generation the assault upon the Bible continues because it is the revelation of Divine truth. The battle takes many forms including questions about the inspiration of Scripture, twisting and confusing what the Bible says, and the argument that people cannot really understand what the Scripture means without assistance to name a few. Add to that, today's busy world keeping many Christians from reading and studying the truth of the Bible, and you have a formula for disaster.

Along the way, the Christian who digs into truth will realize that there are many misconceptions about the ways of God, which the Spirit reveals through the study of Scripture and the prism of personal experiences. The desire from his pre-Christ days to make an idol often carries over into the life of the Christian, since he wants a God that makes sense and that will work in agreement with his thoughts. Truth is the only protection for the Christ follower to mature in Christ, and to see that the ways of God are past finding out, and will often contradict human reasoning. The more his mind comes into agreement with the truths of the Bible, the better his comprehension of the character and nature of the Lord.

The New Testament unveils two enemies of the Christian's growth-in-truth process which disrupts his understanding of God. The first plays a minor role, but must be addressed since it certainly affects in the Christian faith. This enemy is only mentioned once in the New Testament and is a problem confronted in the church at Colosse. A group of mystics entered the church and began to explore what they perceived to be unknown mysteries, which combined Eastern philosophy with Jewish legalism and added a touch of Gnosticism. This strange combination enamored many into false teaching about spiritual matters.

The results were ridiculous notions that diets or rigid discipline could assist a person in becoming more spiritual.

> *These things indeed have an appearance of wisdom in self-imposed religion, false humility, and neglect of the body, but are of no value against the indulgence of the flesh. (Colossians 2:23)*

They taught that receiving complete knowledge of God could lead to spiritual perfection and believed that angels and heavenly bodies strongly influenced what was happening here on earth. (Colossians 1:16, 2:10) (BE COMPLETE – WARREN WIERSBE) Paul let the church know that these deep thinkers were teaching nothing but *philosophy*, which was a danger to truly knowing God.

For by Him all things were created that are in heaven and that are on earth, visible and invisible, whether thrones or dominions or principalities or powers. All things were created through Him and for Him. (Colossians 1:16)

And you are complete in Him, who is the head of all principality and power.(Colossians 2:10)

Beware lest anyone cheat you through philosophy and empty deceit, according to the tradition of men, according to the basic principles of the world, and not according to Christ. (Colossians 2:8)

Certain people have a desire to discover some new truth or to possess a superior knowledge that creates elitism in the body of Christ. This can lead to fad teaching where Christians seek the latest instructor with charisma to make them feel better, rather than to address the call of Jesus to "take up your cross and follow me."

In the last twenty-five years, the church has become more therapeutic with the rise of extremely popular Christian psychologists such as James Dobson, Clyde Narramore, Jay Adams etc., and the pastors of America were jolted to get on board or get left behind. Suddenly, the church was thrust into the world of a better self-image, dysfunctional families, and other psychological terms which led to a more man-centered approach to the church. The next step led to a belief that people need a "professional" and pastors are just not equipped to handle the complexities of modern life.

At an alarming rate, the pulpits began to espouse philosophies that either weakened the power of Scripture, or in some cases contradicted them all together. A cross in the church might offend the unbeliever, or we had better not talk about the "h" word because we want to be positive. We must attract people with their "felt needs" in order to make church relevant. Before long the popularity of these concepts turned sermons into a well-crafted talk, which was more directed at meeting the person's present personal problems than in allowing the truth of the Bible to confront a deeper pressing issue with God, a self-centered life that needs to be crucified with Christ.

This led to the church turning to the marketing gurus of the world to discover what we can do to make our services more attractive. This philosophy of the world did not just creep in; it was invited in with a red carpet extravaganza. In some cases Wall Street and news agencies took notice of this phenomenon where churches operated more as a business than its traditional role in past generations. This, in some cases, resulted in a twisted image of God that equates the prestige of the church as success, and often ignores weightier matters of personal holiness.

Please understand this is not an indictment against every Christian psychologist. The question is whether we start with the Scripture and search for truth, or do we start with what we perceive as a person's needs and look for Scripture to back it up. The problem begins when we question the sufficiency of God's Truth to answer every need and somehow conclude that the problem is psychological in nature, so we must attempt through the mind to arrive at a solution.

A more pressing foe of a renewed mind is what the Bible labels "reasoning" or "imaginations." Both of these terms come from two Greek words, dia = *through* and logizomos = *reckoning, calculation.* You may recognize the second word from which we get our English word, logic. The idea behind both reasoning and imaginations is that a person compiles a list of reasons in his mind and arrives at a conclusion, in this case, about God. Imagination implies that the person in his reasoning is actually deliberating with himself.

There are a number of key illustrations in the Bible where this concept is explained. The rich fool who had so much wealth he did not know what to do, reasoned that he needed to tear down his barns and build bigger, when he should have considered he was going to die and his soul would stand before God.

> *And he thought within himself, saying, "Which shall I do, since I have no room to store my crops?' (Luke 12:17)*

Four men brought their friend who could not walk to Jesus for healing, and Jesus declared his sins forgiven and restored his health. The Pharisees reasoned that a man could not forgive sin and ignored the miracle, never coming to the understanding that Jesus was the Messiah.

> *And the scribes and the Pharisees began to reason, saying, "Who is this who speaks blasphemies? Who can forgive sins but God alone?" (Luke 5:21)*

Even the Disciples of Christ ran into a problem one day as they reasoned among themselves about who would be the greatest.

> *Then a dispute arose among them as to which of them would be greatest. (Luke 9:46)*

Their imaginations led them to believe that one of them would be sitting by the side of Jesus, in the kingdom, in a place of honor, and exercising great power. The logic was based on preconceived ideas of what they had been taught all their lives about leadership, which appealed to the ego and caused them to envy that position. Jesus would confront their misconception with the principle of servant leadership that opposed the best reasoning of the human mind.

The natural understanding of the human thoughts always lead away from God and prevent us from living God's way. This is especially seen in the unregenerate mind as explained in Romans 1:21-22.

> *Because, although they knew God, they did not glorify Him as God, nor were thankful, but became futile in their thoughts, and their foolish hearts were darkened. Professing to be wise, they became fools, (Romans 1:21-22)*

They rejected revelation and chose to devise what God must be like in their own minds and closed their hearts to truth. No wonder God called them fools.

The challenge for the Christian who has left this world of darkness behind him is that he still faces a battle against false reasoning and logic in his new mind. With so much information being pumped into our brain every single day, how is he to know what is true? When we consider the advancement of technology in the information age, it leaves us overwhelmed with all the knowledge at our disposal.

- More than 18,000 magazines and 60,000 books are published every year in the United States.
- The U.S. Postal Service delivers more than 200 billion pieces of mail a year.
- An estimated 62 billion e-mails are sent every day, with e-mail generating about 400,000 "terabytes" of new information every

year (one terabyte equals one trillion bytes). By comparison, a typical academic research library contains about 2 terabytes of information.

- The Internet contains about 170 terabytes of information, which is 17 times more than the Library of Congress print collections.
- About 5 billion instant messages are sent every day.
- The average office printer consumes 24 reams of paper a year.

Data compiled by Brown and Davis from academia, publishers, and other sources. The email and Internet figures are from a study by University of California at Berkeley's School of Information Management and Systems.

Do a Google search on "information technology" and you will have 868,000,000 choices to view.

The Lord's answer for the Christian, who is inundated by too many resources in this age of information, is a simple commandment to "receive with meekness the implanted word, which is able to save your souls.

The Christian life is so intricately entwined with the Word of God and demands we stay that way:

- The Christian is birthed into the family of God by the Word of God .

  Having been born again, not of corruptible seed but incorruptible, through the word of God which lives and abides forever. (1 Peter 1:23)

- God's separation of the Christian as a special object of affection for Himself is accomplished by the Word.

  Sanctify them by Your truth. Your word is truth. (John 17:17)

- The Word provides the Christian instruction and correction in his life.

> *All Scripture is given by inspiration of God, and is profitable for doctrine, for reproof, for correction, for instruction in righteousness, (2 Timothy 3:16)*

- The Christian has confidence in prayer because of the Word.

> *If you abide in Me, and My words abide in you, you will ask what you desire, and it shall be done for you. (John 15:7)*

Yet the question still remains: How is the implanted word able to save the soul? Remember that the mind is the entrance to the soul where ideas and concepts are deposited and transferred into the heart. Out of millions of deposits over the course of a lifetime some are true and a myriad are false. Over time, the false beliefs may become so ingrained in a person that he perceives them to be true. How does a person recognize the difference? Without a foundation of truth from the Bible, he is left to muddle through his own perceptions or rely on the consensus of those in society that he values.

This is a reminder that the more advanced we become in our learning, the greater the chance that our human reasoning is plagued with doubt and confusion about truth. Paul's warning that they were "ever learning and never able to come to the knowledge of the truth" is the indictment against any person looking to understand God with the mind.

Although this reasoning of the mind can be a problem for the Christian, it is certainly not advocating ignorance. It is a plea for truth seekers. The Word of God is the only source of genuine truth and it goes against everything that reasoning suggests. Which of the following truths from the Bible line up with the reasoning of the mind?

- If you want to prosper, learn to give.
- If you want to be exalted, choose a life of humility.
- If you want to really live, die first.
- If you want to be great, place others' interests ahead of yours.

Let me warn you that there is a price to pay for those who determine that truth overrides reasoning. It means that you must become a person who saturates your mind with the Word of God regularly, systematically, and prayerfully. Some are content to run to a favorite preacher or the latest book, but truth seekers stay in the Bible. They explore the Bible not with the intellect, but with the Holy Spirit unfolding the truth of God into the heart. Even when the mind shouts that this defies your better senses, faith clings to the fact that it is truth. The mind is renewed because it knows the truth, and the truth sets it free from the bondage of human reasoning.

For some, this freedom to think with the Biblical mindset of truth is more difficult to obtain, because something has been presented to them in such a persuasive manner over time that they now believe it to be true. They may read in the Bible that it is not true, but these Christians continue to wrestle with half-truths and lies ingrained from their past that hinder progress into spiritual maturity. The Bible reveals this as a stronghold, or a lie that is persistently believed at the expense of truth. Breaking this power in the mind is crucial to the wellness of the soul.

WHEN STRONGHOLDS ARE STILL IN THE SOUL

In your imagination, travel to an ancient time where you stand staring at a castle before you in the distance. The walls tower above you and through the parapets the sun is reflecting off your enemies' shields. The watery moat stretches hundreds of yards out from the massive walls surrounding the entire structure, and promises to be a graveyard for hundreds who seek to pass through. You have been given the assignment by your king to take the city no matter what the cost.

Ignoring the impossibility of the task, you begin to strategize knowing that death is an option, but not failure. You know the water feeding the moat must be diverted and realize even then your army will face a barrage of arrows from enemy archers when you begin to rush the walls. Those who are fortunate to escape the arrows may have huge boulders or boiling water poured down on them through the murder holes. Even if they overcome all these obstacles, the problem of getting past those formidable walls still remains.

This is the image Paul lays for our spiritual warfare in II Corinthians 10:3-5, with the use of "strong holds" depicting a fortress or castle.

> *For though we walk in the flesh, we do not war according to the flesh. For the weapons of our warfare are not carnal but mighty in God for pulling down stronghold, casting down arguments and every high thing that exalts itself against the knowledge of God, bringing every thought into captivity to the obedience of Christ, (2 Corinthians 10:3-5)*

This concept carries us past the normal day-to-day battles the Christian encounters with lusts of the flesh or the attraction of the world. A stronghold is a position that Satan controls which is so fortified that it seems impossible to overcome. As a general rule, they fall into one of two categories:

A sin that is so powerfully ingrained in the believer's life that is constantly used to discourage and defeat him

It is evident when a person comes to know Christ, that an immediate transformation begins and his changed heart has a different attitude towards sin.

> *Therefore, if anyone is in Christ, he is a new creation; old things have passed away; behold, all things have become new. (2 Corinthians 5:17)*

Amazingly, some are instantly delivered from sins that have controlled their lives, and they never look back. For others, there can be a problem that continues to greatly tempt them and seeks to hold them in its clutches. Satan floods the person with guilty feelings and attacks upon his assurance of salvation with convincing conviction that there is no way out.

This is not only true for a new Christian; Satan is a master at uncovering and attacking the weakness of every believer's flesh. Every person has a unique temperament that is a product of his/her ancestors including parents and grandparents. The temperament, according to its own makeup, is prone to a variety of temptations, and the appeal can be so strong that a particular sin may eventually be ingrained into one's character. Once it becomes this stronghold, the Christian fails to see it removed, even though he has confessed the sin and pleads with God to no avail to take it away.

Sometimes we choose to identify such behavior as poor habits or human weaknesses, when in fact, they are strongholds of Satan which hinder the believer from reaching healing in the soul. These range from very serious problems of being slaves to lustful thoughts, or fearful insecurities that lead the person to feelings of worthlessness, to more benign thoughts that keep the person from finding fulfillment in life. Such thoughts can cause the person to believe he is a victim with an inability to ever overcome his problem. At times he will blame his defeated life on parents, circumstances, or even bad luck, not realizing it's his own acceptance of the Devil's lie that keeps him from being set free.

Every Christian has a sin that is a stronghold; however, many are able to hide it with careful manipulation and masking their behavior. Some even display righteous indignation when the wrong of another believer is uncovered, not considering that the only difference is that one sin is exposed and his remains hidden. Make no mistake; sin is like Baskin Robbins' ice cream - a flavor for everyone and when Satan can offer a sin that fits the individual's flesh pattern, the result is bondage.

A promise from God that the Christian is convinced he will never personally possess

Satan would like nothing better than for a Christian to live a substandard Christian life and be unable to receive the promises of God. He convinces the Christian that the promises of God will work for someone else, but not for him. The devil does have a distinct strategy on how to carry out this plan of action.

> *Put on the whole armor of God, that you may be able to stand against the wiles of the devil. (Ephesians 6:11)*

The Greek word for "wiles" is *methodeia* which indicates Satan has a method to entrap Christians, and he is not original. In essence, he has a plan for your life as much as God has a will for you that he wants you to follow.

The most common method the devil uses is to convince the Christian that he is unworthy to receive the promises of God. He will constantly point to the Christian's behavior to prove that God would be unjust to bestow His promises on such a person. Instead of the Christian concentrating upon the greatness of God's willingness to give graciously, he looks at his own faults and failures which destroy his faith. This thought process is so prevalent because most of our society has lived in a performance based acceptance for most of its existence. It is much easier to view God through a works based acceptance, than to see that God's way is grace and He offers his promises to the undeserving.

It is all in your head

The Scripture in II Corinthians clearly shows that there is a warfare going on in your mind. In this battle, there are arguments that stand against our knowledge of God and thoughts that keep us from the mind of Christ.

The Evil One uses this strategy to enslave the people who belong to God and assures them that they are incapable of living the life the Lord intends for them.

Understand that these strongholds can be deposited in the mind by two primary avenues: one voluntary and one involuntary. On any given day, the Christian takes in volumes of knowledge retrieved from dozens of sources including family, friends, and, of course, various mediums. In most cases, the people and sources where this is obtained are not in line with Truth, and in some cases are actually in opposition to Truth. The Bible is not politically correct when it states that the whole world is diseased and under the control of Satan.

> *We know that we are of God, and the whole world lies under the sway of the wicked one. (1 John 5:19)*

Sadly, the Christian is under constant bombardment in the mind by the falsehood of the world, often so subtle that it is undetected. The world dresses it up with terms like "scientific facts" and "history." Even if truth is presented, it is tainted by the world's agenda which opposes Christ. Through the venue of comedy, the world attacks Christian values and questions absolute truth. The thinking of the average Christian becomes so clouded, it becomes difficult to discern between truth and fiction.

This would explain the Barna Group research in 2005 that revealed tragic falsehood held by some who claim to be born-again believers and followers of Jesus Christ:

- 14% believe the Bible is not accurate in all its teachings
- 33% believe if people are good enough, they can earn a place in heaven
- 28% believe Jesus committed sins like other people

If so many can be deceived about the core values of Christianity, how can we expect Believers to have their minds controlled by Truth in the everyday decisions of life? As we become more influenced by the thinking of the world and less knowledgeable of Bible truths, our minds deposit false beliefs into the soul.

Not only must we contend with that which comes at us voluntarily, there is also a weapon that Satan uses against our minds, without our consent. The Evil One recognizes his hope of defeating the Christian by using fiery arrows against the believer.

> *Above all, taking the shield of faith with which you will be able to quench all the fiery darts of the wicked one. (Ephesians 6:16)*

The imagery Paul uses is again from the battlefield where an enemy combatant takes his arrow and dips it in poison before shooting. If he hits his foe in a non-lethal area of the body, the poison will spread and still bring destruction. Our Enemy understands the soul is secure in Christ, but he attempts to fill the mind with thoughts to defeat us in our walk. The future salvation of the soul is guaranteed, but the present success is offered to us by faith in Christ.

These fiery darts are thoughts that come against us without warning and can be blasphemous, lustful, and totally contrary to what we know to be true. They are powerful and cause us to question what we know to be true about God and His ways, as well as throwing the believer into a quagmire of doubt, depression, and anxiety. The hope of the Devil is that the Christian will ignore the shield of faith and not use the sword of the Spirit to protect himself against this assault.

The Christian must realize that the Scriptures are the only means by which the mind can be renewed (Ephesians 4:23), the passion for Christ restored, and the flesh overcome. Each day in humility the believer comes by faith to God for Him to deposit the Truth that will confront the world, and empower his soul with faith to trust God and know He is fulfilling His promises. When the fiery darts of Satan bombard the mind or he is cast down in his soul, the Word delivers him. The Bible contains the arsenal of weapons that God supplies for the saving of the soul.

> *And take the helmet of salvation, and the sword of the Spirit, which is the word of God; praying always with all prayer and supplication in the Spirit, being watchful to this end with all perseverance and supplication for all the saints.(Ephesians 6:17-18)*

It is interesting that the sword of the Spirit is identified as the Word of God. In most cases in the New Testament, the Word of God is from a fairly familiar Greek word, *logos*, but here the term is actually *rhema*, which means a saying of God. Therefore, when we take the shield of faith against the evil thoughts sent from Satan, we must use specific portions of the Word of God that answer the lie with which he is seeking to poison our minds.

The clearest illustration of this principle comes from the life of the Lord Jesus when He is being tempted by Satan in the wilderness. (Matthew 4) Each time the tempter cast a lie at Jesus concerning God or His will for Christ, Jesus simply took a specific portion of Scripture and answered in faith. Each truth chosen was a perfect match to combat the lie, which was actually Scripture Satan, took out of context:

1. Hunger temptation - Deuteronomy 8:3 - Spiritual food

   So He humbled you, allowed you to hunger, and fed you with manna which you did not know nor did your fathers know, that He might make you know that man shall not live by bread alone; but man lives by every word *that proceeds from the mouth of the LORD. (Deuteronomy 8:3)*

2. Pride temptation - Deuteronomy 6:16 - Proper view of God

   "You shall not tempt the LORD your God as you tempted Him in Massah. (Deuteronomy 6:16)

3. Short-cut temptation - Deuteronomy 6:13 - Servant hood

   You shall fear the LORD your God and serve Him, and shall take oaths in His name. (Deuteronomy 6:13)

Even for Christ, this was the only way to combat the attack brought against Him at a vulnerable time and to escape from the power of temptation. It indicates he not only knew the Word, but he knew how the Word applied to the situation he was facing.

Both the voluntary and involuntary deceptions that our minds are constantly receiving must be dealt with at the entrance level of the soul, our thoughts. At times, this means rejecting certain sources of lies because we already know where they are going to take us. This could be questionable types of entertainment or perhaps the latest attack upon Christian dogma by infidels, to name just a few. At other times, the thoughts come from

Satan and we have no control over them, so we must deal with them accordingly.

Previously, we have examined this word "imaginations" which the Apostle now tells us in II Corinthians 10:5 "make up formidable walls that must be torn down" before we can achieve spiritual victory.

> *Casting down arguments and every high thing that exalts itself against the knowledge of God, bringing every thought into captivity to the obedience of Christ, (2 Corinthians 10:5)*

These imaginations in the mind conclude certain reasoning that ignore, justify, or excuse our behavior based on preconceived notions contrary to what we know to be true about God's nature. It is amazing what the mind can conclude even though there is abundant Scriptural evidence to the contrary!

I know that God is love and that He has a special love for His own children.

> *Behold what manner of love the Father has bestowed on us, that we should be called children of God! Therefore the world does not know us, because it did not know Him. Beloved, now we are children of God; and it has not yet been revealed what we shall be, but we know that when He is revealed, we shall be like Him, for we shall see Him as He is. (1 John 3:1-2)*

Yet, often I may be tormented with a flood of arguments to lead to the opposite conclusion. Sickness, financial reversal, or a job loss can suddenly convince me that the Lord is out to harm me. I begin to reason that God is unfair, or perhaps I really cannot trust Him since He has not removed this terrible circumstance. This reasoning that attacks the very nature of God, must be brought down by faith in the Word of God which confronts the false argument.

Some are in such bondage to these imaginations for a lifetime. Certain strongholds are the result of a false idea planted in the mind by an authority who declared, "God could never love you after the way you acted." Other strongholds, more strongly constructed over time as preconceived ideas about God, become ingrained in thought patterns through a warped sense of what God is like.

Then there are those "thoughts" that are in opposition to the mind of Christ. Such thoughts must be taken prisoner and yielded to the mind of Christ. Philippians 2:5-11 reveals that the mind of Christ was seen as Jesus yielded His right to be God, and took the form of a servant in order to glorify the Father by going to the cross. If I claim and exercise my right to anything other than serving God for His glory, then I am not fulfilling the mind of Christ.

> *Let this mind be in you which was also in Christ Jesus, who, being in the form of God, did not consider it robbery to be equal with God, but made Himself of no reputation, taking the form of a bondservant,* and *coming in the likeness of men. And being found in appearance as a man, He humbled Himself and became obedient to* the point of *death, even the death of the cross. Therefore God also has highly exalted Him and given Him the name which is above every name, that at the name of Jesus every knee should bow, of those in heaven, and of those on earth, and of those under the earth, and that every tongue should confess that Jesus Christ* is *Lord, to the glory of God the Father. (Philippians 2:5-11)*

Having the mind of Christ is difficult to practice on a consistent basis. Our flesh screams that we have the right to be treated with respect, appreciated, and even receive certain benefits as servants and children of God. The cross is not welcomed as these thoughts continue to run rampant in my mind which impedes any sense of joy and peace. Is there any way to overcome and bring them into captivity?

The weapons are available

Throughout the Old Testament, God would reveal His power by using ordinary people with unusual instruments to defeat the enemy. With a rod, Moses caused the Red Sea to part for the crossing of the children of Israel, while the water drowned the army of Pharaoh. Gideon had his band of 300 men attack with lanterns inside pitchers and blew trumpets, and the multitudes of the Midianites went down in defeat. Or, consider that Samson, armed with nothing more than the jawbone of a donkey, was able to kill 1000 Philistines single-handedly.

The weapons of our warfare are not physical in nature where we can take them in our hand to battle our enemy. Spiritual battles of the heart and mind demand weapons equal to the task. When arguments are waging war in the mind, convincing us that God is not what He claims to be and calling out to Him is futile, and when everything in our being is telling us to cast off the restraint of the mind of Christ, physical realities are no match.

Praise -The children of Israel found themselves out-numbered by the enemy and the King humbled himself to seek the Lord. With strong faith he consulted the people and decided that the choir would lead the battle. Before a sword was drawn or a life was lost, the choir began to sing praises to Jehovah. The heart of God was moved to act on behalf of His people, and the enemy was slain. While praise is normally the response after a victory, here praise is the *source* of victory for the child of God. Praise casts down the thoughts that are against the knowledge of God.

> *Now when they began to sing and to praise, the LORD set ambushes against the people of Ammon, Moab, and Mount Seir, who had come against Judah; and they were defeated. (2 Chronicles 20:22)*

Worship-David was as low as a man can go. His own son, Absalom, had betrayed him and taken over the kingdom. It would seem that the small band of followers that had escaped with David into the wilderness would have died in a matter of hours. Surely, David should have questioned the ways of God and thought that God had forsaken him. Instead, in an unbelievable act of *worship,* David showed that God had not changed and was worthy of his affection and submission. Worship casts down the thoughts that are against the knowledge of God.

> *Now it happened when David had come to the top of the mountain, where he worshiped God—there was Hushai the Archite coming to meet him with his robe torn and dust on his head. (2 Samuel 15:32)*

Confession-In the end times, the secret to power over Satan is revealed in the blood of the Lamb and the *word of their testimony.* Their testimony was their confession that they belonged to God because they had been purchased by the blood of His Son. When the child of God confesses his relationship to God, he is placing himself in the hands of a heavenly Father who knows what He is doing. Confession casts down the thoughts that are against the knowledge of God.

And they overcame him by the blood of the Lamb and by the word of their testimony, and they did not love their lives to the death. (Revelation 12:11)

Cross -The cross is a mighty weapon to the pulling down of strongholds. When the Christian embraces the cross, he is identifying himself with the finished work of Christ, which is the ultimate evidence of the mind of Christ. This wonderful life of the cross casts down the thoughts that are against the knowledge of God.

> *I have been crucified with Christ; it is no longer I who live, but Christ lives in me; and the life which I now live in the flesh I live by faith in the Son of God, who loved me and gave Himself for me. (Galatians 2:20)*

While this is by no means an inexhaustible list, it places at our disposal the opportunity to attack the strongholds Satan has set up in our lives. Make no mistake, these fortified positions have developed over time, and the Devil will not give up this ground readily. Experience reveals that lies are relentless which demands that truth constantly must be taken into the mind through Scripture reading, memorization, and meditation. These new deposits contradict the previous ingrained lies and philosophies, and over time a mind controlled by the Spirit takes over. Once a person's thoughts are brought more and more into conformity with truth, the ability to set their affections on what matters to God is able to take place.

HEART TRANSPLANT IN THE SOUL

The heart is the crown jewel of the soul for it is the place where love emanates. To say the heart is a primary theme of the Scriptures is a mild understatement, as you examine over 800 references in our English Bible that give us insight into what God says on the subject. To devote only two short chapters of a book about the soul to explore the heart does not serve justice, but hopefully it will whet our appetites to uncover the mystery of desiring to be a person after God's own heart. So let us take the plunge.

The human race finds itself poles apart from God's revelation about the human heart. Most believe people are inherently good and only turn to evil because of injustices in environment, society, or authorities in their lives. That spark of good can be cultivated by education and example to lead us to utopia in the world, if we only will allow people to reach their full potential.

God's view of the human heart is so different. If left to itself, the heart is so far gone it cannot be cured, and eventually will show its true colors in hideous overtures which result in the defiling of a person. The heart cannot be fixed and must have a spiritual transplant that only God can accomplish; again, this is the purpose of the new birth.

> *The heart is deceitful above all things, And desperately wicked; Who can know it? (Jeremiah 17:9)*

> *For out of the heart proceed evil thoughts, murders, adulteries, fornications, thefts, false witness, blasphemies. (Matthew 15:19)*

> *I will give you a new heart and put a new spirit within you; I will take the heart of stone out of your flesh and give you a heart of flesh. (Ezekiel 36:26)*

This puts into perspective the great commandment given to Israel on which Jesus further elaborated in the New Testament, "You shall love the Lord thy God with all your heart…" It is worth noting that this commandment was given directly to Israel and confirmed by Jesus Christ under the new covenant, but this has always been God's desire for the human race. God created Adam for his pleasure and enjoyed fellowship with Adam and Eve in the garden before the fall. We see this later when Enoch walked with God in fellowship, or when God appeared to Abram and promised His blessing if he left the heathen land he lived in to begin an adventurous life with the Lord. This desire for a people who loves Him is culminated in the new heaven and earth when God enjoys the love of His people for eternity.

> *You shall love the LORD your God with all your heart, with all your soul, and with all your strength. (Deuteronomy 6:5)*

> *And you shall love the LORD your God with all your heart, with all your soul, with all your mind, and with all your strength. 'This is the first commandment. (Mark 12:30)*

Although God's design is for people to love Him, this goal was never met under the law by the Israelites as they continually failed to meet the requirement. The only way for this objective to be reached in the New Testament was for God to give a person a new heart after they trust Christ as Savior. So it is through salvation that the miracle of all miracles takes place in the human soul, and gives people the capacity to love God with all their heart. While we learned previously the objective of the mind is to know God, we now discover that the goal of the heart is to love God.

What is love? Ask ten people and you might get ten different answers because the world is very confused about the concept. When we understand that "God is love," (I John 4:8) then our definition of love must be based on the nature of God. God's love is the giving of himself to meet the needs of others even though He knew in most cases He would not be loved back. It is a love that sacrifices his son, a love that is merciful to even his enemies, and a love that seeks those that deserve it the least.

It would be wise to remember that while love is an emotion, it is not always emotional in the truest sense of the word. Love is best shown by actions, not necessarily feelings. Years ago I ministered in a rural community in East Tennessee, which produced a very fruitful church and gave me the opportunity to meet some of the finest of God's people. I will introduce you to two men to whom I had the joy of presenting the gospel.

Bill was a young man with a wife and son who had chosen to live a very sinful life. He actually grew marijuana plants on his back porch and ran with that sort of crowd. One day I was asked to visit him; it so happened that his wife and mother were present, so I decided to present the Gospel to all three. It seemed that the conditions were perfect as Bill listened intently to the Gospel. Then came the special moment when he called out to the Lord. When he concluded his prayer, he jumped to his feet and began to cry while he hugged everyone in the room. It was an electrifying moment of emotion that anyone would be dead not to notice. Unfortunately, Bill followed the ways of Christ for a few months and then drifted back into his former ways.

During this same time period, I visited a successful business man who had attended one of our services. After presenting the claims of Christ, he rejected the offer of salvation so I left him with a reminder to consider the gospel. The next Sunday morning I extended an invitation; Joe came down the aisle and said in a matter of fact way, "Thursday after you left I knelt by my bed to receive Christ; I would like to be baptized." I shared with our church family his desire, but with skepticism thought this could not be real. Joe showed no emotion and it seemed as though he was making a decision similar to ordering a value meal at a fast food restaurant.

How wrong I was! Joe made one of the most drastic changes in his life, and now more than 20 years later he is still growing in grace. Rarely have I seen him emotional, but the radical change in his heart is so drastic that everyone he comes in contact with knows he is a Christian. That he has a love for Christ is evident in his home and business relationships. It would be wise not to judge the heart based on just the surface emotions we observe, since it is a work of the heart where the outward may be misjudged.

In the same manner, the Christian is often confused between that which is a genuine love relationship with Jesus Christ and the desire for romance. Webster defines romance as "a work of fiction stressing adventure and incident: delight in what is fanciful, adventurous, and picturesque." In looking back over 30 years of marriage, there have been times of romance where my wife and I have enjoyed an intimacy with each other that leaves us with euphoric feelings that are too personal to share with others. However, there are times that the mundane causes us to share life that is common and not very adventurous, yet our commitment to love is a bond that keeps us going. In the same way, a heart that is in love with Jesus Christ will appreciate those special times with the Lord, while understanding that the absence of those feelings does not indicate a problem in the relationship.

The important reminder is that the only possible way for anyone to love God is through the new birth, when God gives him a new heart. Then there is a part the Lord plays in developing the soul's love for him. This is not one sided since the person also has a human responsibility, but we must understand the following principles regarding God's work of grace in allowing us to love as well as proving that love.

1. The Lord opens the heart.

   > *Now a certain woman named Lydia heard us. She was a seller of purple from the city of Thyatira, who worshiped God. The Lord opened her heart to heed the things spoken by Paul. (Acts 16:14)*

   Will we ever be able to explain how two people hear the same message, yet one has a heart change and the other one simply carries along the information? Through the years, I have pondered in depth this profound effect as I have observed hundreds who have been confronted with the truth. I have never come up with the formula, and remain constantly amazed when the truth transforms a human heart. I choose to believe in the infinite mind of God; He is more than able to glorify Himself through each one, and really does not owe me an explanation. I will continue to marvel when the change happens.

2. The Lord directs the heart.

   > *Now may the Lord direct your hearts into the love of God and into the patience of Christ. (2 Thessalonians 3:5)*

   It is evident that a heart is able to love God only because it experiences God's love first. The moment I met Christ in salvation I thought I understood love for the very first time and that such love could never be experienced in a richer way. I must confess that through these many years, the Lord now has guided me into a much fuller appreciation and understanding of His love. It is this love which frees the Christian to live in grace.

3. The Lord tests the heart. (Jeremiah 11:20)

   Often, that which is labeled love is nothing more than a selfish desire to meet my own personal needs. True love is sincere (Romans 12:9) and desires to meet the needs of the other person. God knows how to prove my heart's love for Him often through affliction, so my heart will be satisfied with Christ alone. This is actually the only type love the Lord is looking for.

None of these truths remove a person's own responsibility regarding issues of the heart. The Psalmist David, with double emphasis, declared that his heart was fixed which indicates that the heart was fastened down securely or established. (Psalm 57:7) David had nailed down a decision that his heart would recognize who God was, and give Him the praise that was due the Lord. A quick review of Scripture reveals that a believer does possess a new heart, which allows him to make decisions that a person who has not experienced salvation would be incapable of making.

It is also important to remember that a person who knows Christ can actually devote his heart as a sanctuary in which God's presence can dwell. (I Peter 3:15) It was shown previously that the heart is the site where affection originates, and there are hundreds of things to which the heart may potentially become attracted. It is God's desire to have first place in the heart of an individual and that every other love would pale in comparison. This is accomplished as a person understands the value of God and sets Him apart in his heart as a treasure possess.

If our relationship to God is such a priority, it will demand that I guard my heart from outside interference. (Proverbs 4:23) The Christian must view his life as a war for the love of his heart, and that every other affection is a potential enemy. Idolatry is anything that may rob my heart and prevent me from loving God wholly. Even things that others view as harmless perhaps should be sacrificed for the simple reason it competes with my love for the Lord.

When God fixes the heart of a person, then the heart becomes fixed on the Lord. At times there are setbacks, and the new heart is tempted by other loves to forsake the one True Love he has found in the Savior of his soul. The heart will always find that the other loves only offer empty promises. It is amazing that the Christian who has strayed from his first love is able to return to Christ, but even more amazing that Christ welcomes him back with open arms.

LOVING GOD IN YOUR SOUL

When you have royally blown it by leaving your first love and the guilt is so destructive that you want to throw in the towel, what would God say to you? Would He remind you that He had warned you before the incident? Would He try to make you understand the mistakes you made? Would He tell you how disappointed and grieved He was by your actions? While our imaginations run wild thinking of the various possibilities, we actually have an example to look at that reveals the right answer. God would simply ask, "Do you love me?"

The whole sordid mess is told by John in his gospel. In spite of warnings, Peter, as a dedicated disciple of Jesus, cursed and denied he even knew Christ. To assuage his grief he went back to the familiar, a fishing boat where he and his friends were when the resurrected Jesus called on him. There around a little fire, Jesus asked him three times, "Simon, do you love me more than these?" A few days earlier, Peter would have come back with a confident answer; but now he was fearful, uncertain of his own emotions, and quite unable to determine what was really in his heart.

When God looks on the heart of an individual He is looking for love from that person. Jesus even defines that love when He explains, "If you love me, keep my commandments." (John 14:15) The first commandment given to man in the garden was a test of obedience which would reveal whether he truly loved God. From that day forward, God still expects that if a person or people truly love Him, they would obey him. Of course, the Bible reveals that the majority did fail at this requirement and everyone, to some degree, fell short of the ideal. Those who succeeded did so by faith as they walked with his God.

Love is grasping the nature of God

Assuming that what we have said is true and once a person comes to know Christ as Savior he is capable of loving God, does that guarantee he *will* love God? It would seem too easy to answer that question with a simple yes or no and probably would spark debate. A more important question would be, "How can I know for sure I will love God now that I know God loves me?" The first step towards understanding the answer is to be able to grasp a little of the nature of God. Let's take a look at why this is important by taking a look at two groups who confess Christianity, but are poles apart in how they view God.

In 1955, Pastor Fred Phillips formed the Westboro Baptist Church in Topeka, Kansas, which is associated with Primitive Baptists and ascribes to the five doctrinal points of John Calvin. The church believes that the modern homosexual movement is a clear and present danger to the future of America, so they hold demonstrations around the country where picketers voice opposition to homosexuality. Since 1991, they have held over 32,000 protests which are described on their website:

"WBC engages in daily peaceful sidewalk demonstrations opposing the homosexual lifestyle of soul-damning, nation-destroying filth. We display large, colorful signs containing Bible words and sentiments, including: GOD HATES FAGS, FAGS HATE GOD, AIDS CURES FAGS, THANK GOD FOR AIDS, FAGS BURN IN HELL, GOD IS NOT MOCKED, FAGS ARE NATURE FREAKS, GOD GAVE FAGS UP, NO SPECIAL LAWS FOR FAGS, FAGS DOOM NATIONS, THANK GOD FOR DEAD SOLDIERS, FAG TROOPS, GOD BLEW UP THE TROOPS, GOD HATES AMERICA, AMERICA IS DOOMED, THE WORLD IS DOOMED, etc." (www.godhatesfags.com)

On the opposite end of this spectrum is the Freedom in Christ Evangelical Church in San Francisco which states that it desires to reach everyone, but feels its primary mission is to reach out to the gay and lesbian community with the gospel of Christ. The church's 20-point doctrinal statement covers all of the major doctrines which any sound church would believe, but it believes the homosexual lifestyle is completely acceptable to God. By using Bible studies to interpret certain Scriptures, the church believes it proves God is not against homosexuality. (www.freedominchrist-sf.org)

Obviously, both of these groups cannot be right, and in my opinion, both groups are wrong. Of course, I am convinced my belief is based on Scripture, but they would strongly claim the same thing in reference to their beliefs. My purpose is not to debate homosexuality, but rather to examine how these viewpoints are formed by each group's distorted view of the nature of God. The first group believes that God is holy, and that the Word teaches such behavior demands judgment, because it is an abomination. Unfortunately, their view fails to take into account the part of God's nature, that is love which allows Him to be compassionate and longsuffering which can lead those in sin to repent. The second group believes God's love sets them free to participate in sexual relationships that have been taboo throughout church history denying obvious portions of Scripture, thus negating God's holiness. One group suggests God is so holy he hates the people he created in his own image, and the other group indicates God loves so much he accepts that which he declares to be sin.

This one issue is a microcosm of thousands of ways we can form a concept of God that contradicts His true character because we do not really *know* God. Paul prayed that the Father would give the Ephesians "the spirit of wisdom and revelation in the knowledge of Him" (Ephesians 1:17), which is an indication that we are incapable of knowing God on our own. In order to comprehend the nature of God, I need him to reveal his nature to me, and that is done through God's revelation of Himself in the Bible as he dealt with humanity. In addition, I come to know the nature of the Lord through personal experience that is in line with the Scriptures, which is forged by fiery trials which causes me to walk with God. At times, false ideas about God develop in us, and through life events God gives us a clearer understanding of what he is really like. This growing relationship with God allows us to genuinely know him and love him.

Love is resting in God's love

Since childhood most people have heard this simple song:
Jesus loves me! This I know,
For the Bible tells me so.
Little ones to him belong;
They are weak, but he is strong.
Chorus
Yes, Jesus loves me!
Yes, Jesus loves me!

Yes, Jesus loves me!
The Bible tells me so.

Unfortunately, many do not personally believe that Jesus really loves them because of behavior or failures that they experience. For others, the truth may be processed in the mind but it never registers with the heart.

It is very difficult for us to swallow, that God's love for us is born solely out of his gracious nature and there is nothing we can do to merit his love. In a performance driven society where people love us based on our behavior, it is not easy to realize in God's sight, I really do not have anything to offer him that would benefit him. God's plan is for His love to be a magnet that will cause us to love Him back. "We love him, because he first loved us." (I John 4:19)

In order for the heart to love God, then the mind must be processing the proper information from the Word of God into the equation. This is accomplished when we comprehend, that for the child of God every action he takes towards us is an act of love. We understand that when the Father is sending blessings and prosperity our way, but when trials and adversity comes we question God's goodness. When everything that happens in my life is filtered through the principle that "Jesus loves me this I know," then even trials, temptations, failures, and corrections are for my good.

Love loves God in return

Love is a choice. In marriage or parenthood there are certain factors that go into a loving relationship. The following is not an exhaustive list, but most would agree the things mentioned are necessary if love between people is going to be healthy and stand the test of time.

1. Love sees the value of the person you love, which leads to appreciation and expression of love.

2. Love speaks well of the other person to friends and to anyone else that will listen.

3. Love spends as much time as possible with the person you love.

4. Love studies and appreciates the one you love because you want to understand them.

5. Love gladly serves the needs of the one you love.

This is exactly what the Heavenly Father does for his children and what he desires in return. God expresses his love for us, and shows the world we are objects of affection. He longs to spend time with us so he hears and answers our prayer and he knows all about us. He provides our every need. Such amazing love causes us to respond in kind with worship, praise, fellowship, growing in grace and knowledge of him, as well as giving ourselves to serve his cause on earth. When we receive his love our priorities change, as our objective to love God is paramount in our hearts.

Many years ago, I was challenging a person I had just met to bring his daughter to a special children's program our church offered on Wednesday nights. He quickly let me know that would be impossible because as a business owner, he was unable to shut down in time to come to church. He did volunteer his wife to bring their daughter to the program. About two weeks after our visit, this man trusted Christ as Savior and it was one of those drastic conversions. The following Wednesday evening, he was in church without prompting and that discipline has continued for twenty five years. An exciting relationship with Jesus Christ became more important than staying a few extra hours at his business. I cannot resist telling you that his business grew and prospered anyway.

When love for Christ fills the heart, obedience is not drudgery. I have met some Christians along the way, who through fleshly effort follow the rules and even do tasks in the local church, but being around them is depressing. Sadly, what is missing is a relationship, and like Martha, they are distracted by serving instead of communion with Christ. (Luke 10:41) Obedience is a result of love, not a feeble attempt to measure up to God's expectation.

That is really what Jesus was trying to get across to Peter that fateful day on the beach when he asked, "Do you love me?" I am glad to report that Peter got the message. The Peter at Pentecost was not unsure of his affection for Christ or was he reluctant to share the good news with all who would hear. When he wrote to believers, he was no stranger to suffering and urged them to expect fiery trials which were just part of enjoying fellowship with Christ. Once his resolve to follow Christ to death had failed him in a courtyard, but now his love for Christ would cause him to be crucified upside down. For that we do not feel sorry for him, but instead we ask God to give us that kind of heart.

THE FLESH'S DESIRE TO BE KING OF THE SOUL

The tension was so thick you could cut it with a knife. I was the young pastor of a fledgling congregation of 40 people, meeting in a store-front church and conducting my first business meeting. My bride, at the ripe old age of 19, found herself in a position she did not apply for, as First Lady, because her husband had assured her he would be a youth pastor for at least ten years before accepting the role of Pastor. Whoops!

Back to the business meeting, we were actually attempting to adopt a new church constitution. Yes, I was foolish enough to think I could pull it off because after all, I was the *Pastor.* Suddenly, I found myself embroiled with a radical, who was seeking to change every point of the constitution that I had written (actually I copied it from several other church versions), because he thought it gave the Pastor too much authority.

Back and forth we would give our opinions, me behind the pulpit and he sitting in the pew. Everyone knew conflict was brewing and everyone was ready to choose sides. Let's lay it on the table. Are you going to support the new pastor or do you agree with the renegade? Let us settle the issue with a vote.

And then came one of life's most embarrassing moments. Hands were raised, votes were tallied, and it was a tie. Yes, you heard correctly, a tie! Would you like to hear the clincher? My beautiful wife did not vote. Now the real humiliation took place because her foolish husband, with a voice filled with frustration, declared, "Kim, raise your hand and vote."

Now 26 years later, I still remember the shame of my actions and the embarrassment I caused my wife. Many times since then my flesh has gotten the best of me and I have done something stupid, but that incident stands out as how not to conduct a business meeting. No question, there was not a spiritual element in the way I conducted myself that night as the flesh took over my actions. The flesh, or my vain attempts to meet my needs and please God through self-centered efforts, is what hinders obedience in the life of the Christian and brings destructive work in the soul.

In a literal sense in Scripture, the flesh refers to the body of man as opposed to the spirit of man. In spiritual terms the word is used to describe the part of man that wants to protect, promote, and provide for himself the temporal things of life. The flesh is determined to be in charge of his own life and will use whatever means possible to see that his needs and wants are satisfied.

The flesh is determined to control the mind in order to develop a belief system, that allows him to live guilt free while maximizing his pleasure. In addition, the flesh may redefine love so that he may justify wrong actions, or to make love a self-centered action rather than true love which involves a sacrificial giving of self. The flesh is more about taking than giving and is the primary source of destruction to a healthy soul.

For the Christian this unique problem is intensified once the Spirit of God comes to dwell in him after the new birth. A continual warfare ensues because the Spirit desires to be in control to promote the Lordship of Christ, and the flesh is determined not to abdicate the throne.

Galatians 5:17- *For the flesh lusts against the Spirit, and the Spirit against the flesh; and these are contrary to one another, so that you do not do the things that you wish.*

For the average Christian, it is easier to allow the flesh to be in charge than to face the hassle, but the Spirit is not content to allow this to continue.

Now that the flesh has been defined, it is important to know what the flesh does. In general terms, the flesh will take you in one of two directions, either defiance or performance. The flesh does not care which path is chosen, because the ultimate aim is to prevent the Spirit from controlling your life so that you fail to live the Christian life God's way.

Defiance – Galatians 5:19-21

> *Now the works of the flesh are evident, which are: adultery, fornication, uncleanness, lewdness, idolatry, sorcery, hatred, contentions, jealousies, outbursts of wrath, selfish ambitions, dissensions, heresies, envy, murders, drunkenness, revelries, and the like; of which I tell you beforehand, just as I also told you in time past, that those who practice such things will not inherit the kingdom of God. (Galatians 5:19-21)*

When self is not under the influence of the Spirit, a person can live in defiance to God's will which leads to sin. Is it possible for a Christian to be involved in the types of sins that are mentioned in this list? The short answer is "yes" with this clarification: the end of verse 21 makes it clear that a person who does these things will not inherit the kingdom. The word "do" is a present active participle which indicates a continuing practice of these things, which is different than someone who stumbles and commits one of these sins.

In fact, most Christians could identify with at least one of these vices that they have committed or struggled with since meeting Christ. That is not a justification of the behavior, but an honest admission that the weakness of the flesh allows the Christian to be tempted, and perhaps even succumb to a sin of the flesh. A person should not feel superior because he has avoided such sins as adultery, witchcraft, or drunkenness, while he wrestles with perceived lesser sins of envy or strife.

If the flesh is controlling in one of these areas, it would be wise to carefully examine a person's salvation. Such behavior should at least challenge a person's outward assumption that he is saved, but these sins are still ruling in his life. Again, the Christian can commit any of these sins, but if it becomes a life practice, it is a warning of a bigger problem.

When this type of flesh is manifest it is not difficult to identify a Christian as carnal, that is, the flesh not the Spirit is in charge. Many such believers attempt to cease such behavior or cover up the behavior because they sincerely want to gain victory over the problem. The guilt drives them to pray, recommit their lives to Christ, or throw themselves into fervor of religious activity to try to get past the sin. Unfortunately, none of these things bring lasting results.

David-Carnality exposed

David was the "poster child" for the term inconsistency. He was convinced of his salvation, even though he only attended church when some type of crisis would come into his life. He would make a trip down the church aisle to repent at the altar and attend another few weeks before he was out of church again. These escapades continued for several years before I thought he hit his brick wall.

A number of times, I assisted with marriage counseling in an attempt to patch up his marriage and get them on the right path. Each time it involved David's happy-go-lucky lifestyle that would not accept adult responsibility, coupled with his wife's desire to control him, and get things under control. Finally in desperation, she gave up and he was served with divorce papers.

David, whose main goal in life was to have fun, suddenly was faced with the reality of financial hardship, and with the even more depressing fact that he would only see his children every other weekend. For some reason, this time his repentance seemed more real and for a while there seemed to be a noticeable change in his commitment to spiritual change.

He began to actually make a commitment to the things that would bring spiritual growth: Bible study, accountability, prayer. I held my breath hopeful that this time would be different. Wrong. As soon as the dust settled on his divorce, he was back to the taverns looking for pleasure. For the next couple of years, I saw him in church one time just to introduce his new girlfriend.

And then I got the call that shocked even me. His dad called to tell me that David had been arrested for child abuse and he had confessed. A jail sentence was certain. I later visited him in jail and listened to excuses, how he had been abused, and how this just was not fair. He showed little concern now for the spiritual and his preacher was left with the question, carnal Christian or unsaved person?

Performance – Philippians 3:4-6

Many Christians easily recognize the power of the flesh which leads them to sin, but most fail to see a much more sinister manifestation of the flesh. In Paul's testimony we are confronted with characteristics of the flesh that leads to outward behavior that looks wonderful to the natural person. In fact, in some places Christianity applauds such forms of flesh. Before Paul met Jesus Christ, his flesh produced a form of righteousness that caused the world to take notice and the religious community to admire. He was a Pharisee who lived by the letter of the law, whose outward morality and behavior was blameless.

The same flesh that can produce terrible *rebellion* can also make a person *religious.* A key indicator is that he outwardly appears to resemble a Spirit-filled Christian in many respects. He often attends church, serves in some capacity, and is stringent about obeying the rules. The problem is that his behavior is driven by his own power, and when he is recognized for his goodness it only reinforces the ego of his flesh.

Often such Christians can operate for years under the guise of being right with God and even those closest to him do not detect the problem. In time, if the flesh continues to control, circumstances in life will surface to unravel the deception of not being Spirit-led. Usually, it is because he cannot hold to his own expectations of righteousness, and he becomes frustrated trying to measure up. At times this leads to a breakdown of moral failure where the true nature is exposed, or some merely walk away from their religious duties that have become drudgery.

It is sad to see the Spirit begin to work in the life of the flesh-controlled religious person, who ignores His leading in favor of an increased fleshly endeavor. The person thinks if he can get back to a more disciplined life or even add more rules to his behavior he will get back on track. He derives a sense of satisfaction that a recommitment to faithfulness will honor God and God in turn will be pleased with his behavior.

Two key concepts concerning the flesh walk denote behavior that is religious instead of rebellious. The first is that the outward is emphasized to the neglect of the heart. As long as the person is performing well outwardly he is satisfied. Secondly, it is more about performance than it is relationship. The person is much more concerned about what he *does* rather than enjoying his relationship with God.

Linda: The perfect teenager

Linda was raised in a stable Christian home where behavior was strongly emphasized. She lived in the shadow of a brother one year older that did well in school with little effort and who lived an exemplary Christian life. Not to be outdone she excelled in school, learned to play the piano, and never caused her parents an ounce of concern through teen rebellion.

She attended a strict Christian school that made it easier to conform to the rules and a church that held to legalistic values regarding dress, amusements, and dating. In every way Linda was a dream child that every parent would be proud to claim, and it looked like her future was bright.

No surprise that she chose a Fundamentalist college where she could continue to maintain the values that she had all her life and had never questioned. Her gracious spirit, sweet countenance, and many talents caused her to catch the attention of a Bible major named Joe who was heading for full-time ministry. Needless to say, he held more tightly to her strict adherence to rules and it seemed like a match made in heaven.

They started out as an assistant in ministry, but Joe's stubborn ways soon caused them to launch out into a position as Senior Pastor in several very small churches. His demanding ways caused each church to get even smaller, as he would parade out a list of rules that would have to be followed, which would lead him to drift from church to church.

Not long after marriage Linda's health began to decline. She desperately wanted to be the perfect wife, mother, and well adored Pastor's helpmeet. She placed more and more unrealistic demands on herself which led to more complications physically. At times she would think she was having a heart attack which would become a panic attack. On other occasions she would be unable to get out of bed to carry on normal activities or even to take care of her children.

> *Continual trips to the doctor, long hospital stays, and even counseling produced no relief. In desperation she called her former pastor for help. Her husband had no understanding about what was happening, and was convinced she could overcome by prayer and a recommitment to just "doing the right thing."*
>
> *Her former pastor had escaped the bondage of legalism and attempted to introduce her to a grace walk. Unfortunately, all of his recommendations did not meet the approval of her Fundamentalist roots and so the message was lost in critiquing the various authors' stance on issues. What she did not ever come to realize was, that her body was shutting down from the pressure of trying to live up to a standard she was incapable of meeting.*

The Only Solution

What most Christians fail to realize is that every choice the will makes is influenced either by the flesh or the Spirit. The person outside of Christ has only one influence on his choices, the flesh, which makes decisions based on what will protect, promote, and provide for his own needs. In the matter of personal salvation, the flesh will choose religion as the way to make it to heaven because religion gives glory and credit to self. But, when the Holy Spirit enters, He begins to condemn self and reveal that the only way to heaven is through the finished work of Christ.

Through the influence of the Holy Spirit, the will of the flesh is conquered, and the person is able to turn to receive Christ and become God's child. (John 1:13) The new believer immediately has the Holy Spirit take up residence in him (I Corinthians 6:19), and a great battle begins between the flesh and the Spirit for control of the will.

> *For the flesh lusts against the Spirit, and the Spirit against the flesh; and these are contrary to one another, so that you do not do the things that you wish. (Galatians 5:17)*

During Paul's early missionary journeys, he was preaching through the towns and cities in Galatia and the Holy Spirit refused to let him preach in Asia. Next he attempted to head towards Bithynia, and again the Holy Spirit said, "No." So, he went to Troas where Paul dreamed that a Macedonian called to him for help. The conflict concerning his will, preaching in Asia or Bithynia, was surrendered to the Spirit's will to take the gospel to Philippi.

Most Christians would consider this a trivial matter and argue that the desire to go to Asia could not be labeled as a flesh decision. The consensus seems to be that most decisions we make in our life are made without reference to Spirit or flesh. This faulty reasoning concludes that we consult God concerning the "big stuff", but normal day to day activities are left to the individual to decide because there is not a right or wrong in the decision. The Scripture in Romans 8:5 makes this argument clear by revealing that the believer sets his mind to be led by the Spirit or to be affected by the flesh.

The crisis of this viewpoint is the serious consequences of following after the flesh. (Romans 8:6, Galatians 6:8) Such a life is leading to death which I am convinced is not just physical in nature, but is destroying the soul by not allowing the mind to know God and the heart to love God. It is actually an attack on faith as the believer trusts in his own way instead of trusting in the Spirit for every need and decision.

Suddenly, a litany of Bible truths begin to come together to reveal that life in the Spirit brings victory and can only be lived as the Spirit defeats the flesh.

- John 15:4-5-Without me (Christ's life through the Spirit) you (flesh) can do ***nothing.***
- John 6:63-The Spirit brings life, but the flesh has no benefit.
- I Corinthians 15:51 I (my flesh) die daily.
- Romans 8:13-My flesh brings death, but the Spirit can put to death the works of the flesh to give life.
- Galatians 2:20-I am crucified with Christ (my flesh) and now by faith in Christ I am alive in the Spirit.
- Galatians 5:16-Life in the Spirit is the power greater than the desires of my flesh.

It is in our nature to want a quick fix to this battle between the Spirit and flesh, but it never ends. God instructs us to set our minds on the Spirit (Romans 8:5), to continually sow to the Spirit (Galatians 6:8), and to keep being filled (controlled) by the Spirit(Ephesians 5:18). When my flesh is in charge of my will with the desire to meet my needs, fix my problems, and have things my way, there is a destructive force in my soul that cannot be overcome by determination. Might I suggest a simple prayer to God that you could use every day?

Dear Lord Jesus,

> *You purchased me with your blood and I have no right to run my own life. I know my flesh will continue to want to rule, but right now I choose to surrender everything to you. I want to learn to hear and obey Your Spirit in everything so that he might be in control of my every decision.*

It is only through the influence and control of the Holy Spirit that the prosperous soul can become:

- The mind that knows God.
- The heart that loves God.
- The flesh that obeys God.

GPS FOR THE SOUL

If you travel much, there is a good chance you have purchased a GPS location device for your car which allows you to get first hand directions where you are going. I will never forget when my wife purchased a new car in 2002; as the salesman and I sat in the car, and he activated the OnStar device. Suddenly a lady's voice from Canada came over the speaker to ask us how the weather was in Georgia where we were sitting. I was more than a little startled that technology had arrived at the point that she could know where I was sitting, while she was thousands of miles away. Now these instruments are used commonly to let us know where we are, and perhaps more importantly, where we are going.

There is one portion of the Bible which is God's GPS for the soul, and it is chapter six through eight in the book of Romans. Here, a clear road map is laid out for every Christian to possess a healthy soul. The streets and turns are clearer than the little voice that comes out of the box in your car, and it is important we do not choose to take a shortcut or use our own wisdom to design a better route.

> *What shall we say then? Shall we continue in sin that grace may abound? Certainly not! How shall we who died to sin live any longer in it? Or do you not know that as many of us as were baptized into Christ Jesus were baptized into His death? Therefore we were buried with Him through baptism into death, that just as Christ was raised from the dead by the glory of the Father, even so we also should walk in newness of life. For if we have been united together in the likeness of His death, certainly we also shall be in the likeness of His resurrection, knowing this, that our old man was crucified with Him, that the body of sin might be done away with, that we should no longer be slaves of sin. For*

> *he who has died has been freed from sin. Now if we died with Christ, we believe that we shall also live with Him, knowing that Christ, having been raised from the dead, dies no more. Death no longer has dominion over Him. For the death that He died, He died to sin once for all; but the life that He lives, He lives to God. (Romans 6:1-10)*

The theme of this book written to those in Rome is "The Gospel of God," and many times we have misconstrued its meaning. In essence Paul was not writing to share the gospel so that people could come to know Christ, rather he was writing to those who were saved, so they might understand all that salvation entailed. He unveiled God's marvelous grace that had made salvation possible and all that means in this life, as well as the life to come for those who are saved. At the heart of the Gospel is how the saved person is delivered from spiritual death brought on by sin, and how God is delivering them now from the power of sin, as well as the prospect of future deliverance entirely from even the presence of sin.

After using the first five chapters of the book to show how salvation had taken people from the condemnation of sin to righteousness, solely by God's grace and a person's faith in the finished work of Jesus Christ on the cross (4:5, 5:1), Paul then explains in Romans chapters 6 through 8 what the believer's relationship is to sin in this present life. Sin is the destructive force to the prosperous soul so Paul shines light on three areas where the battle is won.

1. *The mind, where my benefits in Christ are explained.*
2. *The heart, which finds it impossible to process my benefits because of the failure of the flesh.*
3. *The heart and mind finding liberty over the selfish control of the flesh.*

Realities Stated

In Romans 6 concerning our standing with God, Paul gives us certain realities. A reality is something that is true whether you believe it or not, whether you practice it or not. There are two realities that are emphasized in these verses by means of repetition.

1. The believer, who by faith has trusted Jesus Christ for forgiveness of sin, *is dead to sin.*

    6:2 – *How shall we, that are* ***dead to sin****, live any longer therein?*

    6:6 – *Knowing this, that our old man is* ***crucified*** *[dead] with him.*

    6:7 – *For he that is* ***dead*** *is freed from sin.*

    6:8 – *Now if we be* ***dead*** *with Christ.*

    6:10 – *For in that he* [Christ] ***died****, he* ***died*** *unto sin once.* (As Christ died, we also died).)

    6:11 – *Likewise reckon ye also yourselves to be* ***dead*** *indeed unto sin.*

We must understand that the Bible clearly teaches that we who have trusted Christ are dead to sin.

2. Since believers are dead to sin, we are also *freed from sin.*

Romans 6:1 reveals to us that the believer is not freed to sin. We are living in the age of grace with more preaching about grace now than in the past. The preaching of grace in the modern world has taught that the believer is now free to sin. Romans 6 teaches us that we are indeed "free from sin."

6:7 – *For he that is dead is* ***freed from sin****.*
6:18 – *Being then made* ***free from sin****.*
6:22 – *But now being made* ***free from sin****.*

The Holy Spirit's speaking emphasizes the realities that the believer is *dead to sin* and *freed from sin.* God repeated Himself to emphasize the fact, that the believer who trusted Christ is dead to sin and freed from sin.

Realities Studied

When studying these realities, we understand that they are *factual realities.* Some parts of our education system teach, that it is not important whether or not the child obtains the correct answer, as long as the student's answer is close to accurate. The concept is that we would not want the child to feel badly about himself because he got the wrong answer. The importance of self-esteem is raised to a level above accuracy. Yet the fact is that 2 + 2 will always equal 4. The same thing applies to these realities stated in Romans 6. No matter what you have been taught or may already believe, it is a factual reality that you are *dead to sin* and *freed from sin.*

As we study these realities, we also realize that they are *present realities.* Many times we read Romans 6 as our position with Christ – what we are supposed to be like. Every time the words *dead* and *freed* are used, they are used in past action. It has already been done. We do not become dead to sin and freed from sin only after we meet Jesus, or after we reach a certain point in our sanctified lives. The day a person trusts Jesus Christ as Savior is the day that he becomes dead to sin and freed from sin.

Thirdly, these realities are *all-inclusive.* I challenge you to find a conditional statement in these verses. They are statements of facts that apply to every Christian. The Word of God teaches these realities about the believer's life; and if you are a child of God, you are included in these truths whether or not you understand the facts.

Realities Simplified

There is some confusion about these realities of Romans 6. Few Christians have a true understanding of this passage. These truths do not indicate that we will not be influenced by sin. Neither does it indicate that we will not have a desire to sin.

In Romans 6, Paul establishes who we are in Christ and establishes that we are dead to sin. Yet struggle follows in chapter 7. We all understand the message Paul is conveying when he writes, "For that which I do, I allow not: for what I would, that do I not; but what I hate, that do I." Paul shows us his struggle in the Christian life. If we are confronted with sin and live in its presence daily, we will be influenced by sin.

Scripture must be rightly divided, and all Scripture must agree with itself. You cannot find anything in the Old Testament that does not conform to the New Testament standard. There are no contradicting truths in the Word of God. The believer's struggle with sin is described in the following passages:

> *Beloved, I beg you as sojourners and pilgrims, abstain from*

fleshly lusts which war against the soul. (I Peter 2:11)

If that lust is a war, a battle, how can we honestly conclude that we have no desire to sin and are not influenced by sin.

But each one is tempted when he is drawn away by his own desires and enticed.(James 1:14)

James is not writing here to unbelievers but to Christians.

There are times that we are tempted to sin.

My little children, these things I write to you, so that you may not sin. And if anyone sins, we have an Advocate with the Father, Jesus Christ the righteous. (I John 2:1)

Why would we need an advocate in heaven if we were never going to be influenced by sin?

For you are still carnal. For where there are envy, strife, and divisions among you, are you not carnal and behaving like mere men?(I Corinthians 3:3)

In I Corinthians 1, Paul addresses this church body as saints of God and holy. Yet the Corinthians were full of envy and strife, fighting with each other, arguing, involved in all sorts of perversion, and other things.

Peter, James, John, and Paul all said that we are influenced by sin and may have a desire to sin. We would be foolish to think that because we are dead to sin that sin does not have any kind of influence on our lives. This struggle will be further explained in Romans 7. What is the clarity of these realities?

Vs. 7 – The word freed means "justified, declared innocent." The believer no longer fears the penalty of sin because he has been declared innocent by faith through the blood of Jesus Christ. "*Therefore, having been justified by faith, we have peace with God through our Lord Jesus Christ"(Romans 5:1) "Much more then, having now been justified by His blood, we shall be saved from wrath through Him."(Romans 5:9)*

> Vs. 12 – "*Let not sin therefore reign in your mortal* [physical] *body.*" The word *reign* is a term which means "sovereign king, ruler." Since God crucified the old man (6:6) with Christ, the lordship of sin has been removed. The unbeliever's nature forces him to sin, but the believer has been brought under a new Ruler, Christ.
> Vs. 14 – "*For sin shall not have dominion over you.*" The word *dominion* means "lord over, rule." Now sin no longer has control over the Christian.
>
> Vs. 18 – "*Being then made free from sin.*" The word *free* means that we have no obligation to sin.

Sin no longer dominates or has power over the person who is now dead to sin, the believer who is now freed from sin. No longer does sin control the believer so that he must obey it. When we died with Christ, the power of sin was loosed. We died with Christ the same way that He died. Therefore, we cannot conclude that we have to sin. That would make us victims. The church should not live in the victimization of the world system saying, "We're just human; we're going to sin." The Bible says that we have been set free from all of that. It is a reality that we are no longer under the power of sin.

RECKONING MY BENEFITS IN CHRIST

We are now made aware of how these two great truths are to affect our thinking. Based on these facts the believer is to relate the truth to his mind by allowing God's truth to overrule contrary thoughts. By choosing to believe the Word of God is more reliable than my feelings or experience, is an act of faith, which conquers the lies that are programmed into the brain.

Our Understanding

Romans 6: 6: "Knowing this, that our old man is crucified with Him." There is a popular teaching that once a person becomes saved he has two natures, the old nature and the new nature, but the Bible is unquestionably clear that the old man died at the cross. The Bible makes a clear distinction between the old man and the flesh and this must be understood in order to live victoriously in the Christian life. Some would suggest that there is no difference between the flesh and the old man, but there is a vital reason why we must distinguish a difference. Jesus Christ did not have an old nature inherited from Adam because he was born of a virgin, but He was flesh.

We must be reminded that the definition for flesh refers to the part of the person, which seeks its own benefit by seeking satisfaction for its own desires and needs. It is because Jesus was flesh that we can be comforted that he was tempted like we are in the flesh, but never sinned. (Hebrews 4:15) A perfect example of Jesus having to overcome his flesh is in the garden of Gethsemane, when he cried out to let the cup of the cross pass from him, but yielded in his spirit to the will of the Father. It was not a rebellious nature that was rising up so powerful that it caused him to sweat great drops of blood; rather it was his battle with his flesh that sought an easier path.

The old man refers to our nature which we possessed before salvation; we were in rebellion against God. We were under the power of sin and dead to God. But at salvation, God killed the old nature and gave us a new nature in the form of the Holy Spirit. Christians are no longer walking in rebellion against God. While there are times when they obey the flesh and seek to meet their own needs and may even sin against God, it is not because they are governed by the old nature because when sin is committed by a Christian he feels guilty, recognizing that he has not obeyed his new nature.

Our Union

There is a union of the believer with Christ when Paul states,*"Knowing this, that our old man was crucified with Him, that the body of sin might be done away with, that we should no longer be slaves of sin. For he who has died has been freed from sin."* (Romans 6:6-7) In simple terms this means the Christian is in Christ, and Christ is in the believer. The result is that the Christian should walk in a new life by the influence of Christ's life in him. The verb form indicates the mood of potential or possibility which reveals the fact that the Christian died and rose with Christ allows him to walk in a new life, but does not guarantee that he will walk in that new life. Later we will find the condition necessary for this transformation to take place is the influence of the Holy Spirit over the person's soul.

We have been delivered from the power of sin and from the penalty of sin. We no longer have to serve sin and are no longer under the condemnation of sin. We have been declared innocent. There are not many Christians who feel innocent from sin, but God declares us innocent. As Christ was delivered from the power of death, we were delivered from the power of sin. As Christ was delivered from the penalty of death by his resurrection, we were delivered from the penalty of sin which has resulted in spiritual life in the soul.

If we died with Christ, then we also were raised with Him. Just as much as we know that we died with Christ to the power and penalty of sin, we know also that we were raised with Him in a new life (v. 4). According to verse 10, our lives are not lived to self but unto God. We no longer live for the things of this world. The old man wanted to live independent and free from God; but God killed the old man at salvation, and now the new person has a desire to live for God. This new desire was created in the soul of the person once God gave him his life at the moment of salvation. (II Corinthians 5:17)

Jesus Christ died on the cross of Calvary. All life was taken from Him – not by others, but because He laid it down. He was placed in a borrowed tomb, and the stone was rolled into place. What did Jesus do in order to be raised from the dead? He is God, and He is the Son of the Living God. But in those three days, Jesus Christ did absolutely nothing to be raised from the dead except to put faith in his Father. He accounted that God would raise Him up by declaring with his last breath, "Father, into thy hands I commend my Spirit." What he did in the physical realm in his willingness to die, and to place complete trust in his Father to raise him back to life, is the example the believer is to follow in his soul. The Christian presents himself to God as a living sacrifice (Romans 12:1-2), believing God will raise him up to a new life. (Galatians 2:20)

Does the Christian have any power to live in obedience and victory over sin? The answer is, "Absolutely not!" He can determine to do better in his own strength, but the end result will always be frustration and defeat. Jesus put himself into the Father's hands, knowing that God would raise him up. Neither can a regenerated person live as God wants him to live; but the same God who raised Jesus from the dead is able to raise us up from a life of dead works to serve the true and living God. It is all accomplished by the greatness of God's power.

Likewise you also, reckon yourselves to be dead indeed to sin, but alive to God in Christ Jesus our Lord. Therefore do not let sin reign in your mortal body, that you should obey it in its lusts. And do not present your members as instruments of unrighteousness to sin, but present yourselves to God as being alive from the dead, and your members as instruments of righteousness to God. For sin shall not have dominion over you, for you are not under law but under grace. What then? Shall we sin because we are not under law but under grace? Certainly not! Do you not know that to whom you present yourselves slaves to obey, you are that one's slaves whom you obey, whether of sin leading to death, or of obedience leading to righteousness? But God be thanked that though you were slaves of sin, yet you obeyed from the heart that form of doctrine to which you were delivered. And having been set free from sin, you became slaves of righteousness. I speak in human terms because of the weakness of your flesh. For just as you presented your members as slaves of uncleanness, and of lawlessness leading to more lawlessness, so now present your members as slaves of righteousness for holiness. For when you were slaves of sin, you were free in regard to righteousness. What fruit did you have then in the things of which you are now ashamed? For the end of those things is death. But now having been set free from sin, and having become slaves of God, you have your fruit to holiness, and the end, everlasting life. For the wages of sin is death, but the gift of God is eternal life in Christ Jesus our Lord. (Romans 6:11-23)

In spite of the simplicity and clearness of these realities which Paul spells out for those who know Christ, the reasoning of the mind will contradict these truths. Often it has been taught that these truths are the position that God sees the Christian in, but the person will not live as though he is dead to sin or in freedom from sin. It is a vain attempt to justify the Christian's inability to live up to the truth by separating our beliefs from our behavior. Paul's answer is straightforward when he declares, "reckon," that is, by faith count this as true even though it seems impossible to live up to its standard.

RESPONSIBILITY BECAUSE I AM IN CHRIST

Stop

We are to stop and understand truth that we have received. Verse 12 helps us understand that we are to have a purpose of heart, doing something within ourselves – "let not sin therefore reign in your mortal body." What is your mortal body? It is your physical body and the word reign means "to lord over." As a result of being dead to sin, we, as believers, must purpose in our hearts that sin is not going to control our physical bodies. We must make that choice, and not every Christian has made that choice. There are some who do not know the facts about their relationship with Jesus Christ, while there are others who know the facts and still allow sin to control them.

This is a personal responsibility. We can pray that sin will not control us. However, prayer will not make God miraculously intervene and cause us not to allow sin to control us. It is not God's responsibility. It is His responsibility to make that possible for us by allowing us to die with Christ and be made freed from the power of sin. God has done His part. God is not going to suddenly make us stop sinning. We have a human responsibility to avoid sin's rule in our lives. That does not say that we will never sin; but we should not allow sin to control our physical bodies.

Some think there are two categories of sin: acceptable sin and non-acceptable sin. There are some sins that believers joke about; however, God says that no sin should control us. We excuse some sins saying, "It's not really that bad. As long as I do my best, God understands. We all have our besetting sins." We must purpose in our hearts that sin will not reign in our mortal bodies.

We are to stop and understand the power of grace.

> *For sin shall not have dominion over you: for ye are not under the law, but under grace. What then? Shall we sin, because we are not under the law, but under grace? Certainly not! (Verses 14-15)*

Grace does not allow us to sin. Nothing is further from the truth. Grace is God's power that enables us to behave as we ought to live, whereas the law could never make us obey. If that were the case, we would not need a prison system today. We would not need capital punishment. We see that in the physical world where we have laws, but the laws do not cause everyone to obey. The law in our Christian lives will not stop us from sinning. Grace has a power of God's energy working in us to allow us to be controlled by His Spirit rather than by sin.

Surrender

> *And do not present your members as instruments of unrighteousness to sin, but present yourselves to God as being alive from the dead, and your members as instruments of righteousness to God. (Romans 6:13)*

The word *yield* means to present to God.

There must be constraint. Do not yield your members as instruments of unrighteousness unto sin. All your members – seen or unseen – should not be used to sin. Our hands have been used to sin; our eyes have been used as instruments of unrighteousness. We should yield ourselves to God. There must be a consecration of our lives to Him. We are new creatures.

The members of our bodies should not be used as instruments of unrighteousness. The word *instrument* means "tool." These are not tools for Satan anymore. These are not tools to be used to promote sin. These are not tools to participate in sin. They are instead tools of righteousness, tools that can be used for God. Our members can be used for sin or can be used for God. The word *yield* in the beginning portion means to keep on yielding. It is to be done continually, day by day. We must yield over and over again. The word *yield* in the latter section of this verse, "yield yourselves unto God," is in aorist tense, something that took place in the past. This indicates that something happened to the believer since salvation. The Christian understands that he was bought with a price and, therefore, gives God everything. It is accepting the lordship of Christ in his life. It is a yielding to God, a complete consecration.

Some Christians experience this yielding simultaneously with salvation. Circumstances and trials may cause another Christian to surrender. This yielding is done only once, giving everything to God knowing that we belong to Him. As Christians, many of us have had a time in our lives where we met with God to give ourselves completely to Him. But we know that it is difficult to continually yield our members to Him. We must choose regularly to surrender our members, on a moment-by-moment basis, as tools of righteousness.

Once we have surrendered, we should begin to serve. In Romans 6:16 we see the law of the servant. "Know ye not, that to whom ye yield yourselves servants to obey, his servants ye are to whom ye obey; whether of sin unto death, or of obedience unto righteousness?" Believers must now make a choice about what we know, to whom we yield, and whom we obey. We can either obey as servants of sin unto death, or we can obey unto righteousness. It is our privilege; we have a choice. We can choose not to yield to God, not to obey God, and live in disobedience and sin. We may also choose to give ourselves as instruments of righteousness. Part of the day we may be servants of sin; the other part of the day we may be servants of obedience.

In verses 17 Paul writes, "But God be thanked, that ye were the servants of sin, but ye have obeyed from the heart that form of doctrine which was delivered you." The words *obeyed* and *delivered* are in past action. As Christians, we have obeyed a message that God has given us. Each day we choose to be the servant to that One we made a commitment to – God. We choose to allow ourselves to be under God's authority, allowing Him to be our Master. We are servants to someone everyday of our lives so the Word teaches us that there is liberty in choosing the right master.

DEAR GPS, DID I MISS MY TURN?

The information in the sixth chapter of Romans is forceful, practical, and makes so much sense when it enters the mind, that we imagine it is going to be easy. Apparently there is something we missed in the instructions once we begin to determine to put those truths into practice. The old enemy of the flesh steps in to volunteer to do what he has been instructed to do, which results in chaos and failure.

The heart's struggle to process the mind's deposit

Out of our standing in Jesus Christ, a struggle is formulated. Even after the mind has accepted that as Christians we are dead to the authority of sin, which has freed us to be able to yield to God's authority, a battle begins to rage in the heart since the flesh is defective. The heart finds it impossible to process these benefits because of the failure of the flesh. What we see described in Romans 7 is the heart frustrated and defeated as the flesh makes an attempt to obey what the mind has accepted, regarding living under the authority of Christ, which has liberated the person from being controlled by sin. This will bring the heart to a point of desperation.

Do a word search concerning Romans 7 and you will find the repetition of certain words uncover a theme.

1. The word "I" occurs 28 times
2. The word "I, me, myself" 47 times
3. The word "law" is seen 23 times
4. The word "commandment" 6 times

The conclusion you will reach is that the flesh, the portion of my soul which seeks its own benefit, decides the way to prosperity is found in will power. "I" can take these wonderful truths Paul has written about, and follow the "law" and be the recipient of a godly life. Instead the exact opposite occurs and the heart, which loves God since it has received his new life in the soul, is defeated and miserable.

The sad reality is that the law can only punish us; it can never reward us. I am not proud of the fact that on more than one occasion I have been pulled over by an officer of the law for speeding. Obviously my flesh was in control at the moment! On the other hand, I obey the speed limit laws more than I disobey, but in almost 40 years of driving, never once has a policeman pulled me over and given me a gift card for *obeying* the speed limit. Imagine the frustration of the man trying to live up to the truth that he carries in his mind about his relationship to Christ, while he knows he loves God in his heart, but his flesh is not allowing him to follow through in his behavior. The law would provide no means or help in breaking him free. Notice all the evidence, which reveals he is God's child and in his heart desires to obey and does not want to sin. The following qualities are indicative of a person who possesses salvation.

1. ***He is decent***

   Paul was a decent man. He was not evil neither wicked. "For we know that the law is spiritual." (v.14) He is acknowledging that God's commandments are a good thing. He also recognizes his own sinfulness (v. 18). Paul is not trying to hide anything from God or to hide his own weakness. Paul concurred with the law about what the law said about him and itself. (v. 16) He did not criticize the law; he agreed with what the law said and actually loved the law when he declares, "For I delight in the law of God after the inward man." (v.22) Paul desired to be the man that God describes in the law. I believe that Paul is giving his own personal testimony. More than anything, Paul wants to do what God wants him to do and to be what God wants him to be.

2. ***He is divided***

   Paul is probably the first illustration of the modern-day term "split personality", in verse 15 we begin to see Paul's division. First of all, he is divided *between his thoughts and his actions.* In his mind he agrees with the law of God, but his flesh leads him to violate God's law by being controlled by the law of sin. His desire is to do what God wants Him to do, but his actions are controlled by sin. He is divided also *between God and sin.* God is pulling one way; sin is pulling the other, and in his soul he is literally being torn apart by those two entities. He also is divided *between mind and flesh.* What he knows and what he actually lives out are opposites.

3. *He is defeated*

In verse 17, Paul reveals that sin is so overpowering as it uses the commandments and the law of God against him, that he feels as if he has no control over his actions. My human-will never allows me to measure up to God by performance, but as we saw earlier our flesh may thrive for a while in its attempt to live godly. (v. 18) He was determined to follow God and His law, but he does not know how to succeed. Paul had learned that no matter how many times he promised to follow the will of God, he was unable to find the strength to actually follow through.

4. *He is distressed*

I almost feel Paul's pain as he cries out in desperation. (v. 24) At that moment in time, he feels like he is the worst human to ever walk the face of the earth. He was distraught by the power of indwelling sin in his life, feeling unbecoming to God and undeserving of His love. We see a man that is distressed. Paul needed an answer. He was not distressed about the penalty of sin nor was he crying out for pardon from sin. He recognized that he had been forgiven and had accepted that forgiveness, but his soul was perplexed by his inability to find deliverance. We find Paul miserable, wanting to be delivered from the power and influence of such a mighty force in his life, longing to find peace in his soul.

5. *He is desirous*

All these things indicate that his mind was settled on truth, and his heart was in love with God, but his soul could not find rest because his flesh remained in control. The important thing is that this is a person with a *right heart,* who is unable to find peace from his *failing will.*

At the beginning of our journey to study the prosperous soul, I shared the story of a number of folks I had encountered who professed to know Christ but their inner soul was a mess. Some of them had missed the truth regarding which we are in Christ perhaps, but most showed evidence of loving and appreciating Christ for salvation in the heart. All of them had one thing in common, no matter the particular sin that was dominating their lives, they attempted to control their own lives and solve their own problems.

Had they looked in the mirror of Paul's experience, where he did the things he did not desire to do and failed to follow through on what he determined to do, (vs.15) they would have seen a reflection of themselves. In Paul's case he was driven to something more, so in his misery he screams, "Who will deliver me from the body of this death?" The one ray of hope for Paul is he finally realizes that, if his soul finds victory it will be in a Person other than himself.

Finding freedom over the selfish control of the flesh

Do you recall that we discovered in Romans 7 that the words "*I, we, myself*" occurred 47 times? The soul of a person never thrives, when the Christian attempts to live out the principles of Scriptures in his own ability following certain laws and guidelines. It is always a lonely walk that ends in frustration. Conversely, in the eighth chapter of Romans, we find the word "*I*" is only mentioned two times while the words "*we, us* and *our*" are written 41 times.

The stark difference is unmistakable, as the person makes a dramatic shift from a lonely walk based on a legal obligation to obey the law of God, to a loving relationship where a Person is forever present to deal with the failure of the flesh. This discovery reveals the only hope for the soul to prosper, is for the will to be conquered by the indwelling Spirit of God, who now resides in the person. This is the end of feeble efforts to resist the selfishness of the flesh, or the empty attempts to reign in sin and bring it under control. Instead, examine how the Spirit renders the flesh impotent.

THE ANSWER OF THE CHILD OF GOD

The Condition of the Flesh

During His agony in Gethsemane, Jesus had warned his disciples that "the spirit indeed is willing but the flesh is weak." Paul, in the previous chapter, had illustrated the weakness of his own flesh as he struggled to measure up to the law of God. Now, he shows the consequences of any believer attempting to live the Christian life through the energy of the flesh.

- 8:3-The flesh can never meet the expectation of the law, which is perfection.
- 8:6-Living after the flesh will lead to death.
- 8:7-The flesh is the enemy of God and must be overcome.

Jesus Christ is our example of how the flesh is to be overcome. It is important to remember the great truth of the incarnation of Jesus. John 1:14 "And the Word was made flesh, and dwelt among us, (and we beheld his glory, the glory of the only begotten of the Father) full of grace and truth." Jesus was the partaker of the same flesh that you and I have, only He was without sin. How was that possible?

It is evident that Jesus pleased His heavenly Father in all things. Through the Spirit of God Jesus ministered, lived sinless, and overcame death. The result is that Jesus judged sin in the flesh (8:3), and he proved that through the Spirit the flesh could be defeated. This is not to say that the Christian will lead a sinless life (I John 2:1), but it does convey that anytime we do overcome sin, it will be only through the Spirit's control in the inner person. This ceases any vain efforts to strive harder at better habits, or the ridiculous notion that a Christian can live right in the sight of God by his own ability.

The Christian must distinguish between walking *after* the flesh and walking *in* the flesh. The term "after the flesh" occurs five times in verses 1-13. The word after means "according to, towards," and Paul indicates that the Christian can be guilty of living to satisfy fleshly desires. Each verse where the phrase is found gives us special insight into this fleshly lifestyle.

8:1-Those who walk after the flesh experience condemnation. That means the believer will suffer the guilt and consequences of sin in this life for obeying the flesh.

- 8:5-Those who walk after the flesh focus their attention on the things that bring pleasure to their flesh. Their goal is to satisfy self.

- 8:12-Those who walk after the flesh do so, despite the fact that they are not obligated to do so. They have been set free by the death and resurrection of Christ.

- 8:13-Those who walk after the flesh will die. The self-life is sin and sin results in death.

In contrast the term "in the flesh" is used in verses 8-9. The word "in" denotes a fixed position in place, time, or state. For someone who only lives in the flesh, it is impossible for that person to please God. Paul is emphatic that the believer cannot be in that position, because the Spirit has taken residence in his life. So while it is possible for the saved person to live to satisfy selfish desires, the Spirit of God within will not allow him to remain in that condition.

The Commitment to the Spirit

There is a reminder in chapter eight of the two laws Paul dealt with in the previous chapter. The second verse reminds us of the law of sin that had enslaved Paul by controlling his body and tormenting his mind. (7:23) The law of sin prevented him from obeying the law of God (8:7) by which, in his mind, he desperately wanted to live and measure up. So now a third law is introduced:

- Law of the Spirit

Simply stated the law of the Spirit is the Holy Spirit working in the Christian to overcome the law of sin and to accomplish the law of God. The fact stated in verse 2 is a guarantee that the Spirit has freed the Christian from the law of sin. The power of the law of sin has been defeated by the law of the Spirit. Now the believer *is not* destined to sin.

The law of the Spirit has accomplished an even greater work. The new law has made it possible for the law of God to be fulfilled in the believer (v. 4). "Might be fulfilled" is a conditional verb that means something has happened to the Christian that makes it possible to live as Christ lived. For the believer who has struggled for years in his soul to live the life God desires for him, this seems too good to be true.

An illustration from God's natural laws may help us understand how the law of the Spirit is able to overcome the law of sin. Sir Isaac Newton is credited with discovering the law of gravity when legend has it that an apple fell on his head. All humans at some time or other have proven this law in a variety of ways, including falling off a ladder or some other humbling experience. For centuries the law of gravity would stand as a law impossible for man to overcome and most would ridicule anyone who thought otherwise.

Then two brothers would come along with a dream to fly like a bird. Of course all knowledgeable people told them that flying was impossible and they needed to stick to the rules. After all, you cannot defy Sir Isaac Newton's law, but Wilbur and Orville Wright proved them wrong. As a result of the two brothers, people were driven to explore a new law, the law of aerodynamics. The rest you might say is history.

Does the law of gravity cease to exist when the law of aerodynamics takes over? Of course not! Neither does the law of sin cease to exist when the law of the Spirit is applied to the life of the Christian. The law of the Spirit allows the soul to soar over the law of sin. So how does this new law work?

- Life in the Spirit

Most Christians have an understanding that the Spirit of God lives in them (I Corinthians 6:19). His presence is the guaranteed down payment on our salvation until we are actually in heaven with God (Ephesians 1:13-14). Again Paul is emphatic that the Spirit of God living in us is proof that we belong to God (v. 9).

What many Christians often miss about the Holy Spirit who lives in them is that the Spirit does not just live *in* the believer, he lives *through* the believer.

But if the Spirit of Him who raised Jesus from the dead

> *dwells in you, He who raised Christ from the dead will also give life to your mortal bodies through His Spirit Who dwells in you. (Romans 8:11)*

The conclusion is that if the Spirit was powerful enough to raise up Christ from the dead then the Spirit has enough might to bring the physical body of the believer to life so that he can lead a righteous life (v.4). This is not an external self-righteousness produced by conformity to people's expectations (Colossians 2:16), but is an internal work in the soul which leads to Christ-likeness in attitude and actions.

It is interesting that as Paul deals with the subject of the Spirit living through the believer, he returns to where the soul is fed, the mind. We reached the conclusion in Romans 7 that this person had a heart whose affection was set on God, even though the heart was perplexed by indwelling sin, and the flesh had made matters worse. So we learn that the problem can only be corrected when the mind of the believer conforms itself to the Spirit. (v.5) How? The Christian begins to think about the things of the Spirit to the neglect of his selfish nature, by concentrating on what the Spirit loves and promotes. The verb indicates a continuous action, which means the Christian is continually yielding control of his thoughts to the Holy Spirit.

The primary way to understand the mind of the Spirit is to ask Him to reveal His truth as we saturate our minds in the Scriptures. This is the "engrafted word" sent to deliver our souls (James 1:21) and is only effective as the Spirit opens our understanding. The result is that the Spirit transforms the mind of the believer. Instead of concentrating on the law of sin, the Christian focuses on the power of Christ at work in his life. He is free from the need to try and measure up to God's standard that he could never reach on his own, and is able to trust the Spirit to produce in him those things pleasing to God. His mind is not driven by guilt and frustration but is established in life and peace.

The practical questions to these truths are important.

1. Does the Holy Spirit live in you? (v. 9)

2. Do you concentrate on the things of the Spirit? (v. 5)

3. Will you by faith, trust the Spirit to put to death the works of the flesh and create God's righteousness in you? (v.13)

There is an important reminder for those who reject the Spirit's influence if the flesh continues to control the mind. "To be carnally minded is death," (v. 6) and it is doubtful that this is referring solely to physical death. After talking to hundreds of people who have ignored the Spirit's life and replaced it with their own selfish desires, I have witnessed deadly results. Minds that are controlled by phobias, depression, and resentment, and hearts that are looking for love in all the wrong places. The battle for the soul is fierce, but the rewards of life in the Spirit are special.

LIVING FOR SOUL CHANGE

Her physical condition expressed the turmoil of a soul ripe with anxiety, nervousness, and fear. Mid-fifties with a loving husband and great kids who were carrying on the faith, she seemed to be abundantly blessed, but for her life, was falling apart. For months she said she needed an appointment to come talk about a "problem", but life kept interfering and we did not meet. Like most people, the misery index had to get higher before she would come for counsel. Then one day, it could be postponed no longer.

She sat across from me with hands trembling and voice cracking as she began in typical fashion with the supposition, "I do not know what is wrong with me." I let her go on for 30 minutes with a confession of how rotten a Christian she was, even though to every outsider she demonstrated the integrity and faithfulness of a devoted follower of Christ. Her conclusion was that although she was doing all the right things, she could not have a joyful relationship with Christ or find any peace. We talked a few minutes about her salvation experience when she met Christ, and it seemed that it was not just head knowledge, but a genuine conversion.

We attempted to go back in life and discover when all this anxiety started. She was raised by a committed Christian family, who was still faithful servants in the church and well respected in the Christian community. At first she indicated no childhood trauma, although she was not extremely popular in school nor did she date much. She was the type who compensated for her insecurities by talking nonstop. Finally, I looked at her and asked her not to say anything for a few moments, but to just think.

After an awkward silence of about 30 seconds, she broke down and began to shake and weep uncontrollably. Then it came out. As a young teen her father had molested her for several years, and for all these years, she had protected him and maintained a typical relationship for her mother's sake. For more than 30 years only two people had known, and now the dirty secret was out to a third party.

A torrent of pent-up emotions escaped and questions began to pour out of her sobbing heart. How could he do that to me? Why did he never confess his wrong to me and seek forgiveness? How could he continue to live a Christian life as though nothing happened? Why did I not do more to stop him? How can people tell me what a wonderful daddy I have, when what he did makes me feel like I am going to throw up? I let her go on without interruption because I felt like the saving of her soul was beginning.

For all those years, Satan had held her in bondage even though she was a child of God. Now the chains were coming off. It was not a quick fix because confrontation, forgiveness, and renewing of the mind would be in her future. The restoring process was so special to observe, and not only was she set free, but so was her dad. The change was noticeable in her spirit, soul, and body.

The world says this form of forgiveness must never be, you must hate your abuser to the death and even then you will not be free. A lie is always well received by the majority, but truth is liberating according to the Master since, "you shall know the truth, and the truth shall make you free." (John 8:32)

Up until now, there may be those who believe the saving of the soul in this life is optional. A person can be saved and his spirit is going to heaven where his body will be delivered from the presence of sin, but the saving of the soul in this life seems unobtainable. Such are basing their assumption on human experience and what seems to be the obvious. There are a lot of troubled souls in our world.

Why should we believe in a God who can keep me spotless against the future day of judgment and prepare a place for me to dwell for all of eternity in His presence, but not be able to deliver my soul in this life? That is a salvation that seems unacceptable to the Christian. We understand the Scripture to be the final authority and confess that "we are not of those who draw back to perdition, but of those who believe to the saving of the soul." (Hebrews 10:39)

We have already seen that this vicious battle for the soul will continue on in this life, but we are not to worry, because the Captain of our salvation has perfect knowledge of our enemy and is more than capable of delivering us. As we rely on his grace and allow the Word to transform our thoughts, feelings, and will, the chamber of the inner soul finds rest. The process at times is agonizingly slow, but we will arrive at the destination: knowing God, loving God, securely surrendered to Him.